An Autobiography of the Enlightened One
Based on His Teachings

Buddha

Recalls and Explains

With Special Emphasis on Meditation; Wisdom; Buddhattva; Enlightenment; Dhamma Chakka Pavattana; and Mahāparinirvāṇa.

Prof. Shrikant Prasoon

Published by

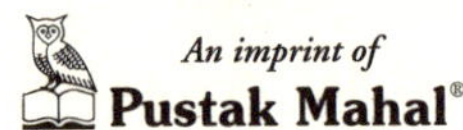

J-3/16 , Daryaganj, New Delhi-110002
☎ 23276539, 23272783, 23272784 • *Fax:* 011-23260518
E-mail: info@pustakmahal.com • *Website:* www.pustakmahal.com

Branches

Bengaluru: ☎ 080-22234025 • *Telefax:* 080-22240209
E-mail: pustak@airtelmail.in • pustak@sancharnet.in
Mumbai: ☎ 022-22010941 • 022-22053387
E-mail: rapidex@bom5.vsnl.net.in
Patna: ☎ 0612-3294193 • *Telefax:* 0612-2302719
E-mail: rapidexptn@rediffmail.com

ISBN 978-81-223-1380-2

Edition 2012

Printed at : Super Fine Binding Works, Tronica City (U.P)

Dedicated to All
Who are striving for
The cessation of mental and physical suffering;
And for achieving Moksha,
the complete liberation
From the cycle of birth-death-rebirth;

And to

P. Sheewale Thero

Shrikant Prasoon

CONTENTS

PREFACE

I have been a voracious reader and have read a lot, almost all the easily available books of Veda Wāngamaya; Samskrit Literature; everything important published in Hindi, which includes the translation; European and American Literature as well as Russian and Chinese; and important books of other religions. After Sanātana Dharma, my interest rests in Buddhism. For this purpose, I established a rich library at home. I had the option of using all the local libraries. This way, different books published in India and also in other countries were easily available to me.

Side by side, I meditate, think and try to co-relate. I prefer thought: refined and sublime thoughts. I never allow worries to creep into my mind. I'm free from worries but my thinking continues. In one of these meditative moods I decided to write a unique book on the Enlightened One. I failed to focus my thoughts on what to write and how to pen my thoughts. I kept on making plans, often selecting a topic and getting into the finer details; yet satisfaction continued to elude me. Therefore I did not begin the book, although I continued writing and translating books and articles on the Buddha and Buddhism.

Then, one fine day, the topic I had been pursuing in my mind occurred to be an Autobiography of the Enlightened One, based on His teachings. I decided to record the events and sermons of the Buddha, recalled, narrated and explained by the Enlightened One Himself. The more I thought about it, the greater was the clarity with which the subject manifested itself in my mind. Beginning with a few related articles, I traversed along the intended course of the subject, through the technique and manner of expressions. Still left a lot to be desired, I finally arrived at this style after experimenting to a considerable extent. I managed to master the style before selecting the teachings of the Buddha, to complete this ambitions project.

Then Shri P Sheewale Theo asked me to write an epic on Buddha in Hindi, which I completed it. Indirectly, it showed me the path.

I wrote, revised and re-revised the chapters to complete the book: **Buddha Recalls and Explains.** The book may be complete but all the teachings of the buddha have not been covered and incorporated, not even the prominent ones. Some very popular teachings have been deliberately left out as most readers know about them in detail. One book cannot hope to cover the vast range of the rare teachings of the Buddha who delivered his sermons for 45 long years in different set-ups and milieu and at distant places.

Encouraged by its appeal, the sonority and sobriety of style, I'm still in the process of reading, collecting and writing. If and when I bring forth another book it will appear as its next volume. I'm sure that I shall not deviate from my original subject: **Autobiography of the Enlightened One based on his teachings**.

I'm sure readers will enjoy reading **Buddha Recalls and Explains** and gain an insight into his message. Some hidden aspects of the Buddha's life and mind will come to the fore.

Note: Since scriptural transliterations are not known to general readers, only ā has been adopted for longer a sound which is otherwise not possible to write in the Roman script. The rest is the same as in newspapers, magazines and general books.

Sarbe Shubhe !

Prof. Shrikant Prasoon
SOLOMON COMPLEX,, Opp. Town Police Station
MOTIHARI 845 401, Champaran East : Bihar
M: 09430994377

E-mail:shrikantprasoon@yahoo.co.in
Website:www.shrikantprasoon.com

ABOUT THE BOOK

This is a much awaited book. Monks, lay disciples and the mass are eagerly waiting for a book that portrays both the inner self and the teachings of Buddha, the Enlightened One. **Buddha Recalls and Explains** is a book written with insight by a tranquil mind that possesses the ability to maintain a balance between attachment and detachment; emotions and reasoning; feelings and intellect; personal life and general teaching. It gives immense pleasure while reading. It gives me a lot of satisfaction to welcome the book with a very brief introduction.

Buddha Recalls and Explains follows a superb technique to express things that were, said more than 2,600 years ago. In a very subtle way, it employs the 'stream of consciousness theory. The book begins when the Buddha has declared and is ready for Mahāparinirvāna (the 1st Chapter) and ends with his Mahāparinirvāna (the last chapter). The middle chapters are what the Buddha recalls and explains. It is a very illuminating, effective and fascinating technique.

The entire book deals only with the concepts and percepts of Buddhism. It is a wonder that no strenuous matter has been incorporated and there is no comparison drawn with the ideas and ideals and teachings of other Dharmas. In fact, no other religion or religious teaching is mentioned in it. Buddhism is the sole subject dealt with.

I consider this to be the beauty and merit of the book and highly appreciate the candid effort of the author, Prof. Prasoon, who has been attending Global Conferences on Buddha regularly for almost a decade. He has absorbed and concentrated on the technique of the Buddha; and has expressed everything only through the teachings of the Enlightened One. He has not used arduous theological issues; although, there were ample opportunities for the Buddha to think of many other things which he may have encountered during his lifetime.

In the modern age when it has become a fashion to create controversy by unnecessarily analyzing 'ancient wisdom' and comparing it with another to prove one's superiority, the inner restraint of the author is praiseworthy. Prof. Prasoon has deliberately and painstakingly avoided such petty methods of garnering 'name and fame'.

Ven P. S. Thero

Sārnāth Centre,
Anagarika Dharmapala Marg,
Sarnath
Vārānasi: UP

E-mail: arya_1891@yahoo.com

BUDDHA RECALLS

Some two months back, I announced my Mahāparinirvān; that I would enter Parinirvān and would not return again. It will be my last and final journey into a state that has neither birth nor death. That day has arrived today. I have been patiently waiting for the day and time. It is not the ripe and right time but this is the day. I shall enter that deathless state today.

Today, when I am finally ready for Mahāparinirvān, the last but greatest journey into the other world, for the final deathless and birth-less state; the events, which came my way during my numerous journeys for the last 80 years, are coming forth like a torrent. I cannot recall them all but many among them are very fresh and lively. I can't shake them off. They are repeatedly striking my mind. They are moving incessantly like the currents of a fast flowing stream of Dhamma, like the rhythmic movement of the eternal Dhamma Parivartan Chakra. These memories are crowding my mind right and left. They are moving from right to left and also up and down, and I can hear their sweet musical sound intently. I see the scenes clearly and the sounds I hear are as natural and loud as they were originally heard. I'm sure, I won't miss a single word but the question is: will I be able to recollect them and repeat to myself in the remaining few hours? I won't. But I can't shake them off. So, I shall try my best to re-live as many moments as I can before I take my 'new journey' into the eternal.

I have no more births so it will not be a new life. I shall simply be and that is all. I will be there forever. Forever living as I am. Enlightenment is so great. We all have a mundane body and the Prāna absorbed fully in the worldly, pleasant, physical and completely mundane. We have to make our Prāna ascend higher and higher in the realm of complete light, total illumination, the realm of Truth and Knowledge where we can be enlightened. It is the enlightenment we need. We need to be enlightened, so that we can be and be forever; so there is no need of further birth and another life. One life with enlightenment is enough.

Universality

Once, I thought that because of this enlightenment, I have left many living and lovely things behind. But that is an illusion. That is the feeling created by Māra. I have left nothing behind. I know I have them all: all the persons dead or living; all the moments sweet or sour; all the feelings pleasant or pinching; I have them all. I have left nothing behind. I'm carrying them. They are in me. They are I. I am those ideas and feelings and emotions and words and moments. They are in me: living and active.

All of them are a part of me: numerous things, events, incidents, persons and ideas are me. It is a very big heap that I have; that I have been carrying this heavy mound. I exist because of them. They have made me. Enlightenment came because I had them; because I had not left them behind. One can't and should never leave the collected and accumulated ideas when one gets fresh ideas. Add something new to the already accumulated ideas to grow rich; to accumulate more; to accomplish something higher. Don't forget. Don't leave behind. Keep them inside. Carry them. Make them a part of the personality, a part of what one is. They make the person, enrich him and enlightenment dawns.

I possess all those numerous ideas and events. They are in me. They have made me possible. I'm the whole; the whole that contains and possesses numerous parts. I'm all. They are all in me. They are mine. They are me. Buddha is but ideas. Buddha declares now that he has become only ideas; abstract ideas that change into concrete reality; and concrete reality that has changed into abstract ideas. From now on, never look for Buddha the person, look only for the Buddha, the ideas. As ideas the Buddha will live with you, in you forever even after the Mahāparinirvāna.

I'm those ideas. The ideas are in me. I carry them. No, they are in me as an integral part. They carry me. They move me forward. They make me utter instructions and teachings. They are the instructions and teachings. The Buddha is in them. Buddha will ever remain in them. They will project and show the real Buddha: Buddha the idea will be with all when Buddha the person has gone out of sight. I carry the ideas, the ideas carry me. I possess the ideas, the ideas possess me. I project the ideas, the ideas project me. I have the ideas, the ideas are me. Look for me in the ideas. The ideas and thoughts will show me as I am.

Light and Truth

The Light and Truth that they possess are my Light and Truth. The Light and Truth that I possess is the Light and Truth of the ideas; my ideas. I have bathed in the Light, the ideas bask in Light; I have found the Truth, the ideas are the Truth. Truth is Light. Truth is in me. I'm Light.

The Light in me is their Light. The Light in them is my Light. No, it's the Eternal Light; Eternal Truth; the Light that was and the Light that will remain; the Truth that was and the Truth that will remain.

The life in me is the life lived during those lively and painful moments. Their pain and vitality is my pain and energy. In the same way, my power, energy and vitality and all the freshness and novelty is their freshness, energy and vitality. They are integral. I'm inseparable from my ideas. I am what I have lived. I am what I have taught.

Variety is the only word that can project me, explain me, represent me and show exactly what I am. The variety is caused by the colours; the ups and ups and downs and downs. I have not always ascended high, I have never continuously descended low. There has been a balance. The hills were high but I had to meet the persons, the suffering masses in the valley. I had to come down to the valleys. I was not always there. I have been ascending very often and very high. That has given colour and added variety to everything that I'm or that I have or that I have given in words and ideas.

It has been a very colourful and lively life. Nature has been with me and I have been with Nature; definitely since my childhood. I know Nature and it has given me immense energy; genuine ideas; fast and fastidious and a variety of colours; sharp and direct insight and serene and lasting tranquility. I'm not one idea, I'm all of them the complete truth and cosmic light.

I shifted my body on the cozy and grassy bed in that lonely forest on a high plain, plateau-like stone. I'm surrounded by many. They have been accompanying me for two months now. I've turned to my left side. The tension has eased out as if there was no tension at all. I have been tense, faced tense moments but have eased the mind out. The tension used to vanish before it could settle in me. I have carried everything except the tensions.

Childhood

I once narrated my childhood, the lovely and lively days, to Sāriputra. Although many monks and other citizens were also sitting around, the enquiry had come from Sāriputra so I think I recalled my childhood for him. At that time, I had said to them:

"O Monks! I was brought up very tenderly, rather highly delicately. My upbringing was exceedingly delicate. In my palace, there was everything. But the real delicateness in my upbringing was caused by the fact that my parents used to have prior information that the young prince could leave the palace. Therefore, many extra arrangements were made for my pleasure. There was a special and very enchanting garden prepared exclusively for me. Besides different fragrant flowers, the garden had lotus ponds. There were three of them: one filled with blue lotus, the other with white lotus and the third one with red lotus. Many other trees were also there, yet I was given only sandal soap and sandal oil for my personal use. The climax was that I was given sandal scent, sprayed on my clothes; and only sandal incense sticks were burnt in my bedroom and living room. My clothes were made up of Benāres silk, particularly of mulberry and *moongā*, coral. Its silk is very cool and smooth and light. In the garden, the *Moulshiri* trees had spread like canopies and the fragrance of *champā* and jasmine filled the place with passion and excitement. Many maids and servants were present all the time and at beck and call to obey my orders.

"On three sides of the garden there were three palaces: specially built for me one for summer, the other for winter and the third one for rainy season. In all the palaces there were special arrangements for music and dance. All the sorts of musical instruments from veenā and sitār to dholak and mridanga were there. Each instrument had a specialist player. Since then, music has been an integral part of my being and language throughout my childhood, youth and the days of incessant journey. My language carries the sweetness of musical refrains, the repetitions; the smoothness and fragrance of flowers; and variety of Nature. My detachment has come from the lotus. I like them all and I have them all. Music has endowed me with the inner ability to know and discern whether the coming sounds are musical or cacophonous. I have enjoyed the music not only of birds but leaves and slow waves too. The flutter of the wings and that of the lotus leaves enchanted me. I used to look at them intently for hours. Those childhood and youthful days around the ponds and in the garden were like gold, silver and bronze and yet soothing. They gave me light, sweetness, smoothness and fragrance. I have been carrying all those along with the unseen pleasure.

"Around the lotus ponds I become a child again; an old child; a child, not of 8 but of above 80. Was I not a child? Always a child! I'm the three: a child, young man and old fellow. All those years are with me. They have always been with me. I have been simultaneously a child, particularly in joyfulness and curiosity; young, particularly for incessant movement and interest in everything and old particularly in experience and wisdom. I am all the three even now."

Oh! The ponds have reminded me that I'm feeling thirsty. I need water. Will I get fresh, clean and cool water here in the forest? Yes, it is possible. A stream flows by it. In the morning we had crossed it. There was only knee-deep water in it.

I don't want to speak. It may break the incessant flow of memorable moments. I make the sign that I need water. Many monks and others too have run for water. The water will or may satiate my thirst. I can wait for water but the moments won't. They are still pouring in as a torrent but are sweet. They have attractions. I like them. I like the life that I have led. I like its moments. I like the teachings that dawned on me and I gave to the people.

BUDDHA EXPLAINS CAUSE AND EFFECT

Two things are simultaneously true: one: there is a cause behind every action and the other: there is an effect of every action. It is a different matter whether we realize or know it. But the effect is there. It is one of the cosmic laws that never changes. It is true of every 'world' and definitely in the world where we live. The result or the effect of the cause cannot be denied.

In our every physical action, there is some subtle force of ideas and emotions. We think first and then do something. The action begins from the thought, and the thought reaches the place of action first and starts a reaction, which is supplemented by the physical action.

The same work done at different times and different circumstances yields different results. Most of the results remain unknown and we are hardly able to realize the complete result because the result of our deeds is not instantaneous. Moreover, we get the accumulated effect of the actions that we have performed. Hence, we are always in dark about the effects of our action. That is the beauty, mystery, illusion and divinity of creation and the cosmic system and law. That gives us freedom to do what we like to do. It gives us equal opportunity to indulge in vices or to be virtuous, to fall down or to rise, to be demonic or sublime.

There are always different actions and reactions in the material world that may be good or evil or may bring good or evil results. One who is not agitated by such material upheaval, who is unaffected by good or evil, is firmly fixed in perfect knowledge.

If one has right understanding and right thinking then one can easily face misfortunes well and change them into good fortune.

The Theory of Cause and Effect

I remember the theory and explanation that I gave the wealthy banker, Anatha Pindaka and his five hundred friends.

At that time, I was staying at the Jeta Vana Monastery near Shrāvasthi. I was sitting on a red-stone seat in lotus posture and was surrounded by a radiant aura of the full moon. That day, the wealthy banker, Anatha Pindaka came to me with a lot of gifts which included flowers, perfumes, butter, oil, honey, molasses, clothes and robes. He was accompanied by five hundred friends. Anatha Pindaka and his friends paid obeisance to me and sat down. They were hovering between heretical practices and Dhamma. I said to them:

"O Disciples! I tell you, nowhere between the lowest of hells and the highest heaven above; nowhere in the infinite worlds that stretch right and left, is there an equal Dhamma. Incalculable is the excellence that springs from obeying its precepts and from virtuous conducts. By taking refuge in the Triple Gem, one escapes from re-birth and the states of suffering. Clinging to the Truth not only endows happiness but also leads ultimately to Arahantship. Following untruth entails rebirth either in the four states of punishment or in the lowest rank and condition."

After hearing my teaching, they finally took refuge in the three Gems: Me, Dhamma and Sangha. This refined them so much that they spent their days in righteous deeds. These righteous deeds will give them a higher and better status in their next birth.

In our subsequent births, we carry on our accomplishment. Those that have refined their inner self will be born with that much of the refined self. Those that have awakened their *Kundalini* in this life need not awaken it in the next birth. In the same way, those that have committed sins and have acquired vices will have to suffer.

Some may be born with good qualities and may yet form a habit of harming others, in this life. Such men will soon enjoy the virtues of the previous life but may then start suffering. All these things happen because of the *kārya-kāran-siddhānta.*

There are two simple ways of getting most out of the *Kārya-Kārana Siddhānta* or cause and effect theory. One is to control one's lust and desires so that one's energy is not wasted on the things to fulfill selfish ends and the other is to direct all the actions towards the common good.

Chetnā aham bhikkhave kammam vadāmi: This includes all kammically wholesome and unwholesome volitions and deeds. Besides volitions, there are other mental factors arising simultaneously in a karmic thought, but volition is the factor that gives moral or immoral significance to an action. Once I told the Bhikkhus while discussing *Kamma.* I said, "It was said that *kamma* should be known, its conditional origin and so forth should be known. What was then said?

It is volition, monks, that I declare to be *kamma.* Having willed one performs an action by body, speech or mind.

And what monks, is the conditioned origin of *kamma*? There is *kamma* leading to the hells, to the animal realm, to the sphere of ghosts, to the human world and to the heavenly realms. It is the effect of the cause, the volitions and the final actions that accumulate and sends one to different lower or higher realms. After creating the cause and after performing the act, the being has no power to change its effect. That is the outcome of the *kamma.*

And what monks, is the outcome of the *kamma.* I declare, listen carefully. *Kamma* has threefold outcome: in this life; in the next life and in subsequent further lives.

Different Cessations

And what monks, is the cessation of *kamma*? Be sure, through the cessation of contact there is cessation of *kamma.* The Noble Eightfold Path leads to the cessation of *kamma.* O Monks! If a noble disciple knows *kamma* in such a way; if he knows the conditioned origin, the diversity, the outcome and the cessation of *kamma*, and follows the way leading to its cessation; he knows the penetrative holy life as the cessation of *kamma*. So, *kamma* should be known, its conditioned origin and so forth should be known.

In the same way, for proper understanding of the cause and effect theory, suffering should also be known. Its conditioned origin and so forth should be known, because suffering is the effect of cause, deeds and actions like bliss. Bliss is also the result or reward of actions.

Birth is suffering; ageing is suffering; illness is suffering; death is suffering; sorrow, lamentation, pain, grief and despair are suffering; not to get what one wants is suffering; the five aggregates subject to clinging are suffering; and even the brooding over previous sufferings is also suffering. It is definitely because of the effect of the previous actions that one suffers. If actions are purified and are moral and righteous, there will be total or partial cessation of suffering depending on the degree of purification and wholesome deeds.

And what monks, is the conditioned origin of suffering? Remember it; craving is the conditioned origin of suffering.

And what Monks, is the diversity of suffering? The diversity of suffering depends on the intensity of suffering and the intensity of feeling the suffering. There is intense suffering and modest suffering; there is suffering that fades slowly and there is suffering that fades away quickly.

And what Monks, is the outcome of suffering? Suffering manifests itself in different ways. Some persons are overwhelmed by suffering; the mind is in the grip of suffering; one grieves, laments, moans, weeps, beats one's breasts, strikes one's head against hard objects; and also becomes deranged; loses one's mental balance.

Often people search for the remedy of their suffering in the outer world. One searches for the remedy while the remedy is within him; in his right thinking and right action.

And what monks, is the cessation of suffering? Be sure; the cessation of craving is the cessation of suffering. The Noble Eightfold Path leads to the cessation of suffering. That takes away the painful effect or pain creating effects of unwholesome deeds. The cessation lies in changing one's acts to wholesome and righteous actions: right view, right intention, right speech, right action, right livelihood, right effort, right mindfulness and right concentration.

If a noble disciple knows the cause and effect; the unwholesome deeds and suffering in that way, if he knows the conditioned origin, the diversity; the outcome and the cessation of suffering and follows the way leading to the cessation of suffering; he succeeds in getting rid of suffering; in ascending to the state of sainthood–Arhantship and is freed completely and forever from the cycle of birth, death and re-birth. So, follow the Noble Eightfold Path meticulously well and always for permanent happiness.

Mind it: *sarve bhawantu sukhinah* discards none, and 'you' are not excluded. You are a unit of the '*sarve*', and if all are pleased, healthy and happy; and have no suffering, then, you are one of them. You are happy and healthy and have no suffering. Suffering will come to an end."

BUDDHA RECALLS AND EXPLAINS

I have just finished a long discourse. I finished it with: *kusala vipākāni pancha vinnāni*. The entire gathering is silently brooding over it. I'm myself waiting for them to absorb the complete meaning, its full impact. I have a question in my own mind: will they reach to the most pertinent question? It is: Which are the states that are indeterminate?

When as a result of good *karma*, *kammam*, the moral action, having been stored in the outer world, visual cognition will rise accompanied by disinterestedness, the real impact of *uppekhā* which is a psychological term and signifies neutral feelings, will become manifest. It finds its object in something seen, contact, feeling or perception in the form of disinterested thinking and self collectedness.

The mental condition, which is neither pleasant nor unpleasant, is born out of contact with the appropriate element of visual cognition. The sensation, which is neither easeful nor painful, is born of contact with thought; and the feeling born of contact with thought is neither intimate nor totally alien. It is this feeling that is there in it.

The perception, the perceiving, the state of having perceived, the thinking, the cogitating and also the reflection are born of contact with the appropriate element of visual cognition; and it is this thinking that is there in it.

The Skandhas

On such occasions the thought is ideation as the sphere of mind. The *skandha* of intellect and also the persistence of thought are all in that simple state of 'self-collectedness' and disinterestedness.

They must realize that the *skandhas* are four; the spheres are two; the nutrients are three and the faculties are also three but the contact counts as a single factor. All these states are indeterminate.

I am sure they won't include *gyāna* and *māgga*: Knowledge at its extremity has conception: *vittakko* and the path at its extremity has cause: *hetu*. Hence, their mind will not consistently include them in their conceptual activity. The thought to them may appear casual, but it is effective.

In *vittakko,* the mind is working towards an end: good or bad. Neither *vittakko* nor *amoho* is a possible constituent in a cognition, which is inefficacious to produce good or bad *kammam*.

The gathering is still silent. The quietude is soothing and revealing too. Some of them have their heads down; some are looking nowhere, but most of them are looking intently towards me in expectation. They expect me to say something more. They know each word of mine is meaningful and has a lot of denotation and connotation. They are always expectant. They need explanations. My words give them faith and confidence. Even those who are looking nowhere are expecting me to say something more that can throw more light on the topic.

What I like, in them is their inquisitiveness. They are always inquisitive, including Ānand, who usually listens to my complete sermons; and they are quite large in number: non-countable in terms of quantity and very deep and illuminating in terms of quality. Their interest is in the quality, which brings them to me in large number on *Purnimās,* which are quite different. They hardly get enough open space to sit in open areas like this. I see them everywhere.

Usually, I deliver my sermons to my disciples but *Purnimās* are different. People from far and wide come to listen to me. It is one such *Purnimā*. I'm waiting for a question to come from some corner. They seem to be at their wit's end: what to ask? Who will ask? It will satiate their expectations and thirst if I restart the sermon on my own as it will shed more light on the indeterminate. I shall raise the question myself and provide the answer. I start speaking:

"Which are the states that are indeterminate?

"When as the result of good *karma* having been wrought, having been stored up in connection with the sensuous universe; auditory cognition, olfactory cognition or gustatory cognition arises accompanied by disinterestedness and having as its object; a smell, a sound, or taste; or cognition of body arises accompanied by ease and having as its object something tangible, then there is contact, thinking, feeling, perception, ease, self-collectedness, the faculty of ideation and vitality. These or whatever other incorporeal, casually induced states there are on the occasion; these are all the states that are indeterminate.

"The cognition of something tangible has a positive and pleasant concomitant if the *karmas* are good but unpleasant if they are bad; and the comment it evokes is not less so. Touch or body-sensibility is the one sense through which the four elements without and within the individual come into direct contact. Other cognition is secondary, in as much as the other senses are *upādā,* derived. They are akin to balls of cotton wool on four anvils, deadening the impact of the hammer. In touch, the wool is beaten through, and the reaction is stronger. Nevertheless, the ease or the distress is so faintly marked, that the cognition remains indeterminate. Good takes effect in ideation: *kusala vipākā manodhātu.*"

I have stopped talking. Silence prevails. Satisfaction has covered all the faces that I can see at a glance. It is another place to stop. In the distance on three sides, I see one cart each loaded with food for the gathering. I signal Ānand to get the food distributed to and among the persons gathered there. I pull the pillows closer to relax for some time.

The monks are doing their work with the help of the householders. Most of them are eager to serve the people. Service to others is an inborn quality in this part of the world. All have the instinct to serve. There is another quality here that is very prominent. It is friendship. People make friends and maintain the friendship through their life. Oh! It is amazing. Determination and dedication are very common features here. In this context I once drew the attention of both the lay men and the monks towards friendship. I abundantly made it clear, with whom one should make, keep and maintain friendship.

Seven Qualities

I remember clearly what I said at that time. I have not had the opportunity to repeat it at different places yet have repeated it in a few discourses. Now, the disciples will repeat it in the near future and also in the remote future. I said:

"O Monks and Householders! A friend should be followed if he possesses seven qualities. What seven qualities? The following seven qualities:

First: A friend gives what is difficult to give.

Second: A friend does what is difficult to do.

Third: A friend patiently endures what is difficult to endure.

Fourth: A friend reveals his own secrets.

Fifth: A friend keeps a friend's secret as his own secret.

Sixth: A friend does not abandon a friend in misfortune.

Seventh: A friend does not despise another friend because of his loss.

Friendship should be maintained with such a person who possesses these seven qualities."

It is fresh in mind and comes to my mind because I see here among the congregation today some such friends who have been coming together and have attended many gatherings to listen to me. It is not the discourse that I'm thinking about. I am thinking about those persons and their lasting relations. *Mitratvam amritam santi.* Friendship is like nectar: sweet and lasting.

BUDDHA EXPLAINS SIMILARITY IN DEEDS

I turned my head when I heard: 'Ānand salutes Tathāgata!' Yes, it was Ānand, fresh and energetic. I blessed him and invited him. He sat at his usual place in the half-lotus posture. I felt a fading twilight. Darkness was slowly growing wider and deeper. A monk came, saluted me and Ānand and placed a clean brightly lighted lamp at its designated place. Some late birds were returning home thanking all else with their peculiar chirp. I have been always familiar with all sorts of chirping. Chirpings for meals and in fear are quite different, the latter is quite sharp.

'Tathāgata!' Ānand whispered.

'Well, Ānand! Do you want to say something?' I asked and prompted him to open and empty his mind. Questions must be answered, otherwise the mind remains pre-occupied and pleasure is drastically reduced.

'Yes! Tathāgata!' Ānand started speaking in a voice that had neither passion nor showed impatience. I have always appreciated his patience. 'Today, I went to Migasālā for food. I sat down on the seat specially prepared for me. She came, paid due homage and sat down on one side. She was unable to control her curiosity. She eagerly said:

"O Venerable Monk! I have my doubt. When my father Purāna departed, he was a celibate. He had no lust and no sensuality. The Blessed One declared at that time that he had attained the state of 'once-returner', and that he had been born among the Tusita Devas. When my uncle Isidatta departed, he was not a celibate. He was leading a contented married life. At that time, the Blessed One declared that he too was a 'once-returner' and had been reborn among the Tusita Devas. I have my doubts. I am unable to understand how both of them had the same status though their life and deeds were different."

'I tried to answer her but since I have my own doubts, Migasālā was not satisfied with my answer. Kindly explain this so that I may someday satisfy her curiosity.'

Doubts Weaken

Ānand was silent and before the silence could grow deeper I started explaining the obvious that eluded them. I said:

'Those that have doubts and are suspicious will not get peace in life. It is one's deeds that are important not our judgment. Anyone can pass a judgment that one is inferior and the other superior. Such judgments will cause pain and suffering to them for a long time.

'One who has heard my teachings, has a keen understanding and attains a temporary liberation of mind, surpasses another and excels. The Dharma-stream carries him very far, untroubled and obstacle-free. These differences are known to only a Tathāgata, the Perfect One, the Blessed One.

'Therefore, one should not be a hasty critic of other persons and should not pass judgments every now and then. It is not that clear and that easy. One who passes judgments harms himself. I alone, or persons like me can judge someone and pass judgment that holds true.

Six Types of Persons

'Ānand! There are six types of persons in the world. One is gentle. He is a pleasant companion. He is happy and keeps others happy.

With such men, monks gladly live together. But such a person has little learning and has not heard the teachings. He has no understanding and has not attained even temporary liberation of mind. Such a person is set for decline after death. He is not set for progress. He will deteriorate and not rise higher.'

'O Ānand! There is one who is gentle. He is a pleasant companion. He is happy and keeps others happy. With such men, monks gladly live together. Such a person has great learning and has heard the teachings. He has a keen understanding and has attained temporary liberation of mind. Such a person is set for progress after death. He is not set for decline. He will not deteriorate and rise higher in the next life.'

'There are beings with inferior dispositions and beings with superior dispositions. Those with inferior dispositions associate with, approach to and frequent among beings of inferior dispositions. Those with superior dispositions associate with approach to and frequent among beings of superior dispositions. It has been so in the past and will be in the future. Such a person has little learning and has not heard the teachings. He has no understanding and has not attained even temporary liberation of mind. Such a person is set for decline after death. He is not set for progress. He will deteriorate and not rise higher.'

'Likewise, there is another person prone to anger, greed and lust and from time to time these qualities rise high. Such a person has great learning and has heard the teachings. He has a keen understanding and has attained temporary liberation of mind. Such a person is set for progress after death. He is not set for decline. He will not deteriorate and rise higher in the next life.'

'There is another person prone to anger and greed. These qualities often rise in him, particularly verbosity. Such a person has little learning and has not heard the teachings. He has no understanding and has not attained even temporary liberation of mind. Such a person is set for decline after death. He is not set for progress. He will deteriorate and not rise higher.'

'In the same way, there is another person prone to anger, greed and lust and from time to time these qualities rise high, particularly verbosity. Such a person has great learning and has heard the teachings. He has a keen understanding and has attained temporary liberation of mind. Such a person is set for progress after death. He is not set for decline. He will not deteriorate and rise higher in the next life.'

'Other persons may criticize. The critics will pass their unwise judgments that this one has the same qualities as that one. Why then, is one superior and the other inferior? But one who has heard the teachings and acquired much learning, possesses a keen sense of understanding and has attained temporary liberation of mind. That one person will excel upon the other because the Dhamma stream carries him along. Only a Tathāgata, a Perfect One is aware of the difference or that of similarity, if there is one. I alone or one like me can judge people.'

Ānand had his answer. Satisfaction brightened his face in the dim light coming from the earthen lamp and the tenth day moon. He rose and after seeking permission and offering salutation, went away. I gazed at the stars that were increasing in number every moment in all directions.

I remained there for quite a long time without moving, without thinking. I was only gazing mostly at the stars, mostly around the Ursa Major to the Pole star. Their twinkling light is soothing and satisfying. Suddenly, I marked one thing. For its verification I sat down and slowly moved my head and eyes in one direction at a time. I repeated it for hundreds of times but I could not find **any three stars in the whole of sky in a straight line**.

What a wonder! What a miracle! Trillions of stars, almost infinite in number; here and there; side by side but no three stars in a straight line. I kept on gazing. First I reclined, then fell asleep.

BUDDHA EXPLAINS WORLDLY HAPPINESS

I think primarily on two problems. One is to wipe out the incessant pain and suffering from life and the other is to see happiness all around in all living beings, which is best projected in human beings.

These are basically only one problem; or at the most, two sides of the same rough plank. There is no single plane that can make all the planks smooth. No, there are countless variations of different type and nature. One 'idea' can't uproot all the ills. Geographical conditions differ; the social set-up has many layers and there are numerous mental modifications that keep on coming in disguise. Moreover, human beings create more problems than they can solve. They make their own changes. Humans can never follow the dictates truthfully and honestly. They perceive the meaning in different ways and analyze them for their own gain. Therefore, all the generalities are made personal and all the personal feelings are by nature, generalized.

Misery is there and it will not be completely erased as it is very deeply rooted in existence, kindness, co-operation and saving others for our own safety. It is the law of co-existence. Not only that, even our deeds will not be free from mistakes and vices. Hence, the law of the *Karma* will also affect life. So, one should not imagine a life without pain or suffering. Yes, the pain and suffering can be easily minimized.

Man is a peculiar living being. Every little thing is a problem for him, big enough to cause suffering including walking, eating and sleeping or a rotten fruit, falling hair, no hair or lots of hair; and no problem is big for him, not even the loss of crops or ravaging fire or not even death and *Nibbāna.* Man can feel pain in every little thing and can sacrifice life easily. It is all in the mind. Only the perception makes the difference. Only an individual approach is meaningful. If the mind is clear and pure, life will be free from pain and suffering.

Happiness

So, once there was a very dense gathering. The number of householders was many-fold higher than that of the Bhikhus, and people from many corners and every strata were sitting at every place and in such a disciplined way that movements were not hindered. I wondered how such disciplined person can lead an undisciplined life doing excesses in almost every walk of life and inviting all sorts of pain and misery.

Then a householder, Anāthpindika by name came to me, saluted and requested for my sermon in a whispering voice. I smiled my acceptance. He was satisfied and took his place. I addressed the whole gathering:

"O Householders and Bhikhus! I shall explain material and worldly happiness which you want and which you lack. Happiness comes from satisfaction and satisfaction comes from the fulfillment of desires. Fulfillment of desires is based on right and balanced deeds. So, happiness depends on the degree of righteous deeds and satisfaction in life. It depends on time and occasion and the type of sensuous pleasure that a layperson enjoys.

A householder can obtain and feel four kinds of happiness. What are those four types of happiness?

The first one is **the happiness of possession**.

The second one is **the happiness enjoyment**.

The third one is **the happiness of debt-less-ness**.

The fourth one is **the happiness of blamelessness."**

Personally, I don't like to keep on speaking continuously without taking breath and without giving the audience time to understand and absorb the full effect of the statement. The faster it will come from my mouth, the faster it will enter their ears and the faster it will be lost because the mind can't retain all that comes to it. The mind has a habit of selecting the ideas to be kept, categorizing them and arranging them in different order and places them according to their importance. The preference depends always on the personal liking and needs of an individual. So, I waited for some time, giving temporary relief to the audience and their minds to think on their own, about the four points I had placed before them. Then I began again in my known confident voice, making the pitch, rise and fall, erasing the possibility of being monotonous.

'O Householders! What is the happiness of possession? You must understand it clearly for you possess something and you are happy. You get something and you are happy. But when you lose something you are unhappy. When something is denied to you, you are unhappy. Happiness is very flickering and very momentary.'

'O Householders! In the mind of a lay man I, my and mine play prominent roles. I'm the owner. It is my house. These fertile lands are mine. Such thinking gives them both satisfaction and happiness. It is the happiness of possession. Those who think like that have earned wealth and property by working and striving hard. They have acquired them with their mind and hand. They have earned them with the sweat of their brow. It is their righteous wealth earned through righteous means. They have performed meritorious deeds. They are proud of their possession. This sense of possession gives them happiness and joy. A lay man is never free from that sense of possession. Bhikhus are different. They don't think like that. They have earned merit by a different method. Their possession and satisfaction and happiness are entirely different. Lay men rightly hold the view and get happiness.

'O Householders! What is the happiness of enjoyment? Householders acquire wealth by energetic striving, physical labour, mental agility, helping others and by obtaining help from others, by co-operation or solitary effort. One amasses wealth by the strength of one's arms and mind; earns a lot by the sweat of one's brow; gains wealth righteously by righteous means. Such a householder enjoys his wealth; performs meritorious deeds with the amassed wealth. He spends it on his family members, on his neighbours and relatives. He donates a part of it for the welfare of others. He gets pleasure out of it. He is happy. He is happy to see his family members, friends, relatives and others happy. He experiences happiness and joy in many forms and ways. He enjoys sensuous pleasure as well as mental satisfaction. That happiness encourages him to strive more, to do more meritorious deeds and to make many more living beings happy. O Householders! This is known as the happiness of enjoyment.'

Happiness without Debt

'O Householders! What is the happiness of debt-less-ness? When a family is not indebted to anyone to any degree for anything, they are free from worries and anxieties. One must consider it barring the debts in the form of sympathetic and compassionate love shown towards any member of that family. It is a debt of a different kind. Though, one must try to pay it back in sympathy and compassion, love and assistance, support and co-operation, yet it can never be fully paid back. But there are many worldly and material debts that are slow killers. If a householder and the members of his family are free from any such material debt; if he owes nothing in worldly terms; if he has not taken loan in any form; then he and his family are happy, satisfied and contented. They feel relaxed and fearless. They face others boldly. They are not afraid of anyone or anything. They strive for their own sake or the sake of meritorious deeds. They don't strive to pay any debt. They are free from that painful worry. They are happy. That family is happy. O Householders! This is known as the happiness of debt-less-ness.'

I remained silent for a few minutes. I was thinking of the blessed souls that are free from debts. It is a blissful life. One has done a lot, helped many persons. He has given a lot to others but has taken nothing from others. He owes nothing to a person. He won't ever be shy of meeting a person. Those that are in debt rarely forget the debt. They shake like banyan leaves when they see that person from whom they have taken a loan. The fear is: if he asks me to pay back in the presence of so many persons, my weakness will be known to all. He becomes restless and till the other person is there, he thinks of him and about the possible insult. It is pain of the worst nature. Therefore, it is a boon to be free from debts. I know, it is a great pleasure to be free from debts. I concluded my short sermon with the analysis and explanation of the fourth kind of happiness.

'O Householders! What is the happiness of blame-less-ness? Many people are blamed for this misdeed or that crime; this failure or for that lapse. They get no respect, neither from the society nor from the family members. They are the persons of negative thinking and negative deeds. But there are persons who think in a positive way; adopt righteous means, are ethical and perform meritorious deeds. They neither think ill nor do ill. They are respected both by the family members and the society. They are blame-less. They are free from worries. They suffer the least. They think of the welfare of others and their own welfare is guaranteed. It is because of the law of *karma*. One will plant a mango sapling and will get mangoes. Such a person is endowed with blameless conduct of deeds, word and thought. All such persons experience happiness and joy. They are blessed. A blameless life is bliss. They are happy. O Householders! This is called the happiness of blame-less-ness.'

'O Householders! These are the four kinds of happiness that a householder, a person who enjoys sensuous pleasure, a materialist or a worldly person feels. They achieve the pleasure depending on time, place, occasion, perception, intensity of feeling and approach. From now on, be wise and happy and enjoy the blissful state of happiness: the bliss of possession; the bliss of debt-less-ness; the bliss of enjoyment and the bliss of blame-less-ness reasonably and ethically.'

'Be sure to strive hard. Do a lot of physical labour and perform many meritorious deeds. Earn, spend and be happy. *Sarve bhavatu sukhinah*!'

'One should look inside for real pleasure; lasting happiness; total wisdom and continuous progress. They have a wrong notion and look outside for everything, fail badly to get it and hence are aggrieved. One must search for a thing where it may be, where it is. Searching at the wrong places will not give access to the thing being searched.

'One who meditates searches at the right place and gets what he is looking for. Meditation gives insight and keeps one tranquil. After great and continued meditation one grows bigger, stronger and wiser. His strength increases after every such effort.'

'We cannot control time but we can adjust ourselves to be always in time; with time and even very often, ahead of time. If it is practiced strictly well then we can become timeless in time. Our fallacy is simple: we don't understand it; we don't believe it; we have no confidence in our inner strength and we seldom grow in a rational and calculated way from the inside, which is the only growth known so far.

Plants grow from inside; the branches come out from inside; leaves and flowers and fruits come from inside. The pulp in a fruit and even the rind on stems and skins on fruits come from inside. Yct we ignore our inner strength.'

They don't realize the full impact of my words and ideas. They don't meditate; they don't dive deep and stay inside longer. They did not realize what I meant when I said, 'Being dispassionate, one becomes detached, through detachment is liberated. When liberated there is knowledge that he is liberated. He now knows that birth is exhausted; that the life has been lived wholly; that what had to be done is done, and there is nothing to be done on this account.

Yes, this is the time for Nirvāna; Mahānirvāna; Parinirvāna; Mahāparinirvāna. Birth is exhausted, there is no further birth. Death is exhausted, there is no further death. Arrival and departure are exhausted, there is no more arrival, again and hence no departure. Life has been lived wholly. What had to be done has been done. There is nothing left to be done on any account. I have attained that state of no return. I will depart today but will never return.

BUDDHA EXPLAINS DARKNESS AND LIGHT

I have seen the plain surfaces where every type of plants, trees and crops were grown and all sorts of living beings lived, played, ran and galloped on it; I have seen river banks and sandy beds where melons and cucumbers grew in plenty; and I have seen sharp and steep edges on hills, mountains, banks and mounds where fall, cuts and wounds are easier. A bit of light is needed to tread on plain surfaces; a bit of control and precaution is needed to move along the banks, but a lot of control and balance and light is needed to pass by the edges. Mental control, physical balance and the light of knowledge are a must for remaining free from harm at the extreme edges or to cross them over.

The Relationship between Darkness and Light

I was engrossed in thought. I felt something out of the ordinary. Yes, evening had come, light had gone. The moon was yet to rise. It was thin darkness all around, growing thicker. I saw people coming. I surveyed the place and found many persons sitting in every direction. Some were standing, some were searching for suitable places to sit and some were coming through both the paths that came up to that plateau-like hill.

For different reasons and purpose, light and darkness are needed and essential. Light helps us in seeing both the obvious and things that are behind curtains, out of sight, very far. For them, the light of knowledge and insight is needed. In place of acquiring worldly riches some people acquire, accumulate and use this light. They are wealthier, more accomplished and of more essence.

That day, I preferred to address the monks who were sitting closer to me. They outnumbered the householders who still kept coming. But the sermon was for all, for all human beings. I have never kept my sermons confined to a region, a sect or a faith. The Eternal Truth is for all to know and follow. I began:

'O Monks! There is a deep relationship between darkness and light. There is no place which is absolutely dark and there is no place where there is absolute light. They co-exist like other things and other living beings. Darkness follows light and light follows darkness. Who is following whom? Both are leading and both are following.'

'O Monks! In relation to darkness and light, there are four kinds of persons in the world. Who are those four kinds of persons in relation to darkness and light? They are:

First, who **move from darkness to darkness**;

Second, those who **move from darkness to light**;

Third, those who **move from light to darkness**;

Fourth, who **move from light to light**.

'And now Monks! Who are the persons who move from darkness to darkness? Who are they that get no light? They are the persons who are not refined. They make virtually no use of their mind. They show no progress. So, they are both mentally and physically crippled. They are selfish, full of lust, jealous of every one and have a lot of anger that they express every now and then. They use abusive language and beat their own wives and children. They are outcasts in the society and even in their families. They get virtually nothing, they possess nothing, they give nothing and they perform no meritorious deeds.'

'They are confined to darkness. Such people spend their life in thick to thin and thin to thick darkness. They perceive no light. There is no light in their life; no light in their mind. They don't grow. They know no culture. They make no progress. They die in almost the same ignorant state in which they were born because they make no improvement, neither inside their selves, nor in their family conditions, nor in social-status. They are definitely re-born in even lower families and as in their first, so in their next lives, they live in a hell-like place, dipping lower.

'And now Monks! Who are the persons who move from darkness to light? They are the persons who strive, often strive hard to be refined, to grow both from outside and inside. They acquire knowledge and worldly possessions. They help others and obtain help. They are both caring and careful. They prefer to be in the middle, perform their duties well. They know their responsibilities and fulfill them. It makes no difference to them if they are weak, ugly or crippled. They compensate for it with diligence and wisdom. They never lag behind. They manage their self, time, family and actively participate in social works, charitable deeds and works of public welfare. They disregard their weaknesses and shortcomings. They are the truly successful persons in the society for they engage in good conduct of body, speech and mind. Such persons are definitely reborn after death in good and moral families. They ascend upward to a heavenly abode.'

'And now Monks! Who are the persons who move from light to darkness? After death, some persons are reborn in a high family, get better education and opportunities. They aquire a handsome and strong body and riches: land, cattle, silver, gold and associates and relatives. But in place of using them in meritorious deeds they become victims of immoral and amoral physical pleasure, luxury, sycophancy and deceitful deeds. They lose the strong pedestal on which they were standing. They fail in every task and at every point and fell into a hell of their own creation, the worst hell.'

'They descend to the darker regions of life. They get a lot to be happy but they waste all: self, wealth, character, morality and other good possessions. They engage in misconduct with their body, speech and mind. They are fallen people, *patit*. And so, such persons are reborn after death in lower world, low family and face hell-like situations.'

'And now Monks! Who are the persons who move from light to light? There are some persons that are reborn after death in a high family obtain better education and opportunities. They acquire a handsome and strong body and riches: land, cattle, silver, gold, associates and relatives. They work hard and grow well. They refine their wisdom, mind, thinking and deeds. They grow incessant from inside and outside. They use their wealth and other possessions in the best way possible, in meritorious deeds and for the welfare of the family and society. They look after their family, dependents, employees, friends and relatives in the best possible way. They grow from strength to strength because they engage in good conduct of body, speech and mind. And so, such persons are reborn after death in a higher world, in a grand family and enjoy a heavenly life doing greater deeds of people's welfare. They are usually called lucky but they possess greater qualities and have been doing meritorious deeds from many past lives.'

'Be sure to strive hard to come out of darkness and move towards light both in the outer world and inner self. Do a lot of mental labour to gain immense ability so that you can perform many meritorious deeds. Light your own life and the life of the others, and be happy. *Sarve bhavatu jyotirmayāh*!'

With this I stopped speaking but the people and monks gathered there waited for a long time digesting what I had said and in expectation that I might say something more. But I preferred to keep mum, for it was a lot for them. I had given them some solid ideas. Had I said something more, that would have turned them to that new statement; if I kept mum, they would certainly be thinking on the statements given earlier. That would be more beneficial. In my philosophy and way of thinking, the benefit and welfare of the masses is more important. For them I came out, for them I went into penance and for them I keep on thinking ways and means of teaching the path to them. All living beings are the centre of my thinking, core of being and living, and their painless living is my sole aim. Let all attain light: worldly, inner and celestial: *jyotita ho jag sārā mana sārā*: let there be light everywhere and in every heart.

BUDDHA EXPLAINS INSIGHT AND TRANQUILITY

One must have the power to see beneath the surface. To see the outer layer is a common ability of the eyes but to know the qualities of things, persons and events is a gift of knowledge and thought. Only he possesses the insight who has the thinking and meditative power. Insight is, in fact, the power of seeing into and understanding things. It is imaginative penetration into others' mind and events. It is the deep and practical knowledge; a personal view into anything; awareness of others' and one's own mental condition and inner thinking; the wisdom inside the principles of the things that happen. The highest quality of insight is 'enlightenment'. In that sense, insight is direct learning without the process of trial and error. The enlightened one knows with extra effort.

In the same way, one must have inner tranquility, calm, peace and ease. A tranquil mind has won over all the trends and common feelings that spoil the peace and pleasure of life. He who possesses tranquility has obliterated the lust, anger, jealousy, fear, physical pleasure, sensuousness, ego, the sense of being great and powerful and all sorts of attachments. He commits no unjust or sinful or unethical-immoral action. He has no craving. He needs no material wealth. He has so much of inner power that he can satisfy his hunger without eating a thing or by eating anything: grass or leaves, cooked or uncooked grain, fruit or root. There is so much of inner energy that it easily gives ease to body and mind, and that is an important reason that such a person feels no pain and no agony, and is never perturbed at any event or by any word.

Inner Power

Inner tranquility of mind is *ajjhāttāin chet-samatā*; it is *antah gyāna*, deep concentration and full mental absorption and the highest wisdom *adhipannā, dhamma-vipassanā*. It is higher knowledge that discerns mental formations and checks them: *sainkhār aparigāhaka vipassanāna*.

Insight and tranquility are inner power, in fact, great possessions of a person. It is thousand times greater, higher and deeper than worldly possessions. The initial state of insight and tranquility makes a man human; the next stage gives him the sublime quality; the third state is divinity and the final state is enlightenment.

The aim of human life is to attain insight and tranquility and finally, enlightenment. The opportunity to serve and work for others; and to acquire knowledge and wisdom is to move on the way to attain the most needed: insight and tranquility. These qualities can emerge only when the mind and deeds are pure and free from attachments and desires. Only such persons can become *Arhant* and attain enlightenment.

It was a distinguished gathering of only monks: sophisticated, refined, cultured, wise and thoughtful. The very appearance of the monks was heartening and satisfactory. They were sitting peacefully in a half-meditative state and yet were eager and enthusiastic to learn more. Their inner being was completely open to me. I started telling them:

"O Monks! Listen to me attentively! I will explain both insight and tranquility. These are very important and definitely essential for monks.

Who possesses tranquility and insight? All persons cannot achieve the peaceful state of tranquility, nor acquire deep insight. It is a specialized trait. To see in a special way, *vipashyanā*, and know the things that are usually unknown. To think and feel the truth that is not apparent and to get *param shānti*, complete peace. From among those who have refined their knowledge, feelings, emotions, thoughts and deeds, there are different categories.

A person **attains internal tranquility of mind, spiritual and almost eternal, but does not gain the highest wisdom of deep insight into the things**. The knowledge remains almost at the surface while peace settles inside the heart and mind.

Another person, O Monks! **Gains the higher wisdom of insight into things but does not gain internal tranquility of mind**.

Yet another person, O Monks! Who **gains neither internal tranquility of mind nor the higher wisdom of insight into the things**.

But there are a few persons, O Monks! Who **gain both the internal tranquility of mind and the higher wisdom of insight into thins**.

O Monks! Who are the persons who attain internal tranquility of mind but do not gain the highest wisdom of deep insight into the things. They are the persons who have not grown up from inside in a balanced way. They did strive very hard, with concentration and diligence, to get something which they got but something else remained out of their sight, out of their mind and out of their effort. They did not get that. Hence, they lack it. So, whosoever lacks the insight into the things must go to one who has gained internal insight and great wisdom. They should place before him some questions for enquiry like:

What are the inner elements of formation?

How can formations be seen?

How can formations be explored?

How can creation be discerned from inside with insight?

The person with wisdom and insight will reply him adding his own knowledge and experience in this way: Such and such are the inner elements in every formation and creation. In such and such ways formations can be seen. In such and such ways formations can be explored. In such and such ways creation can be discerned from inside, with insight. The person will follow the instructions to the letter and keep on gaining in insight. One day, that person will gain both the internal tranquility of mind and insight into the things.

O Monks! Who are the persons who gain the higher wisdom of insight into things but do not gain internal tranquility of mind? They are the persons who are still restless, still not free from attachments and are easily influenced by the Mārā who lulls them towards pleasure and luxury. They are the persons who have not grown up from inside in a balanced way. They did strive very hard, with concentration and diligence, to get something which they got but something else remained out of their sight, out of their mind and out of their effort. They get it but they do not strive hard enough to get rid of the attachments and desires, so they do not gain the internal tranquility of mind. Such persons who have not as yet gained tranquility of mind should go to a wise one who has gained both wisdom and insight. They should place before him some questions for enquiry like:

How does the mind actually function?

How can the mind be controlled and steadied?

What are the modifications of mind?

How can one get rid of the modifications of mind?

How can one get the needed concentration?

How can one be composed?

The person with wisdom and insight will reply him adding his own knowledge and experience in this way: Such and such are the ways the mind actually functions. Such and such are the means by which the mind be controlled and steadied. Such and such are the modifications of mind and such and such are the ways to get rid of the modifications of mind. By adopting such and such methods, one can get the needed concentration and be composed. The person will follow the instructions to the letter and keep on gaining in peace of mind. One day, that person will gain both the internal tranquility of mind and insight into the things.

O Monks! Who are the persons who gain neither internal tranquility of mind nor the higher wisdom of insight into the things? They are the persons who have not grown up; who did not make efforts to grow from inside and to get wisdom or to be free from lust and attachments and to get inner peace and ease. They are still living on the lower plane on which they were born. Such persons should go to a wise one who has gained in both insight and wisdom. They should place before him some questions for enquiry like:

How can formations be seen?

How can the mind be controlled and steadied?

The person with wisdom and insight will reply him adding his own knowledge and experience in this way: Such and such are the ways the formations can be seen and explored and the mind can be controlled and steadied. If that person uses his ability he can follow the instructions and start growing from inside. The very beginning of the inner growth is so amazing and uplifting that once a person gets it he won't abandon the practice and steadily keep on growing. It will take time, diligence and concentration, but that individual will also get insight and wisdom.

Gaining the Two

O Monks! Who are the persons who gain both the internal tranquility of mind and the higher wisdom of insight into things? They are persons of higher wisdom and developed perceptions. They have won over every worldly attraction and attachments and have almost perfect peace of mind. They are assets to other human beings. They can remove the pain and suffering of others by guiding them through thick and thin and by inspiring them to come out of the worldly web. They should be requested for instructions and sermons and their words and ideas should be followed meticulously.

O Monks! I advise you to examine your inner self and to do the needful."

I saw satisfaction on the faces and eyes of the monks. I felt the immense growth in their inner self. I closed my eyes to keep them inside and silently blessed them all.

I closed my eyes but I was awake, fully awake. This inner awakening has been with me. I realized it only under the banyan tree; the Bodhi tree where I became the Buddha. That changed me into energy. I became power. That gave me light. I became Light. It is inner power and inner light. It is the light without heat. It is soothing illumination.

BUDDHA EXPLAINS BEAUTY AND UGLINESS

For the wise and enlightened it may be different but for the lay man, life is always a puzzle. They lack the wisdom, the purity, inner moral power and the strength of pure living, yet they try to explain everything: the broad and obvious as well as the intricate and mysterious. They fail and hence, give many simple, complex and incongruous explanations. Their analysis is also either very plain or awkward. All ideas find acceptance and all ideas are denied. Acceptances have their own logic and denials too are not illogical. There is hardly one word or one sentence or one idea that can analyze and explain all seemingly simple and bizarre incidents that keep on happening here and there.

What is easily forgotten is the reaction. People forget their own reactions and seldom consider the reaction of others: human and non-human; the great phenomenal earth and Nature. They don't consider their own actions of the past and the present. They forget and try hard to forget what they did to themselves, their family, fellow human beings and other living beings. All those actions, have reactions and their effects. Therein lies the meaning. If all those actions of all those men were to be taken into consideration, it would be an impossible task, for the universe is big and numerous actions are taking place at every place throughout the universe. But if it is analyzed, the meaning will be crystal clear. Some semblance can be found. It is possible, at least for those who have wisdom and subtle insight into things, mind and universe. That way, one can draw some definite conclusions which will explain many things; and life will not remain a puzzle. A simple and balanced understanding of life will help one live a satisfactory and pleasant life.

At that time, I was staying at Savatthi. One of my favourite places was Jetā's Grove. It was Anāthpindaka' Monastery. It was in the open and there was no dearth of water, air and sunshine. I liked the three. I liked the people who were very diligent and intelligent too. All these combined together had a great appeal but the strongest reason behind my stay there was the peaceful milieu all around. Here, flowers bloomed in thousands. The fruit orchards remained laden with ripe and unripe fruits. A host of children always played on and around the trees. Some people were always found reclining under the shady trees. Nature loves her children and provides each needed thing. Men destroy them and suffer. Man has failed to keep intact what Nature has provided in abundance. There is an imbalanced competition of consuming and finishing the natural wealth in haste. This will cause immense suffering and agony to the coming generation. Nothing else but Nature can save all living beings. **Sabbe shantthu sukhinah!**

Sāriputra came to me and informed that Queen Mallikā was coming with her maids to meet me. I knew Queen Mallikā. She was the chief queen of King Pasenadi of Kosala. She is still alive and fulfilling her promises. She is a living force. She is now worshipped but when she came to meet me, she was known mostly for her queenly status and ugliness. Now, she is respected for her humane qualities. Her ego, anger and harsh treatment have been replaced by humility and compassion and helping and sharing nature. People never talk of her ugliness any more. Her meritorious deeds have covered her physical, mostly facial ugly appearance.

Though they had de-boarded the royal chariots yet the flag led them towards me. It was a colourful crowd. The royal march was visible from a long distance. It was almost a caravan moving at trained feet. It looked like someone proceeding towards a big cultural function. It was moving towards me at a calculated pace.

Kings and queens have a habit of showing their wealth and power. It satisfies their ego. They feel elated. They are too attached to their royal living that they seldom think of life as a whole. They don't realize the value of and peace in detachment. They won't accept that the riches do not belong to them; that only purity, morality and meritorious deeds are theirs, their saviour and heaven here and hereafter.

The caravan of Mallikā had come closer. She was herself in the lead. It was easy to recognize her. She was formally greeted and welcomed and was given a seat. The vanity of royal living have no place in the monastery. All living beings are the same. The difference of wealth and position have no meaning here. The difference in work culture and habit; mental agility, skill and growth and pure and compassionate deeds are given preference but it was hardly shown in the outer behaviour. On the other hand, the respect and honour bestowed upon such pious figures clarified the acceptance. There was no denial. Negative attitudes should never be encouraged.

In fact, the place was fit for meditation and penance. King Bimbisār had admonished me from going for penance in the very prime of youth that my age was not ripe and mature for penance, that I had the option to take it up at a later stage but they are the people who love wealth, power and luxury. But I knew if something is not done, if one won't do it during his youthful days then he cannot perform such mentally and physically taxing deeds when he is old, weak and withered.

Mallikā is also of that tradition of royal display. Her attire expressed a lot of the attitude. The maids endured her behaviour over their disciplined ways and tired faces. Though, they were in royal service, there was no happiness, either on their lips or in their eyes. A certain dryness characterized them.

Oh! Yes! She was ugly! Very ugly! So ugly that neither the expert and rare make-up nor heavy regal garments were able to hide it! Not only the contours and skin but also pox-like deep spots, tanned and burnt blemishes and specs along with the marks and scars were like stigma. But it had not affected her royal gait and grace. She was composed and circumspect and yet worried.

Worries and anxiety are the worst curses of royal life. No one seems to be free from them. The faces express the inner agony and longing. They are so much worried about the unseen and unknown contingencies of the future that they fail to do justice to the needs and demands of the present. The present becomes painful for both the palace and people, which is easily extended to future. The past has not been happy, present and future are also rendered painfully hard under the unbearable load of worries and anxieties; fear and demands and fear of demands.

Mallikā bowed to pay homage before she sat and tried to appear relaxed. Her maids presented gifts and donations in covered shallow large dishes of brass, (*parāt*). In order to make her feel really relaxed, I said:

"O Mahārāni Mallikā! How is King Pasenadi! How are the people of Kosala! Is there peace, health and happiness? Is there no threat?"

"O Shākya Muni! The mass is working and living in health and happiness! The just King is looking after all and ruling with kindness and compassion! There is no immediate threat of any attack; neither in aggression nor in defence! It is peace, toil and pleasure!"

She tried to bring a smile on her face but failed. Her inner pain prevented the projection of any pleasure or satisfaction. I had to know the reason of her arrival:

"O Mahārāni Mallikā! Then what is it that has brought you here? Why did you leave the queenly abode and stately facilities?"

"O Shākya Muni! No one could satiate my curiosity. I find four categories among women. I want to know what is the cause and reason behind beauty and ugliness; and affluence and poverty. The restlessness caused by that curiosity has brought me here. I want to know."

She didn't speak in a crescendo as women usually do. They talk non-stop. On the other hand, Mallikā stopped after every question to see and gauge the effect on the large audience and me. Then, she started again:

"How and why are some women in this world ill-formed, ugly and also poor? Why are they destitute with little or no wealth: neither of physique nor of mind; neither material nor spiritual, neither power nor influence?

"How and why are some women in this world ill-formed, ugly but rich? Why do they have great wealth? Why do they enjoy great prosperity and influence?

"How and why are some women in this world extremely beautiful, attractive, rather enchanting and graceful but poor? Why are they destitute with little or no wealth: neither of physique nor of mind; neither material nor spiritual, neither power nor influence?

"How and why are some women in this world extremely beautiful, attractive, rather enchanting and graceful, and also rich? Why do they have immense wealth too? Why do they also enjoy great prosperity and influence?

At least one thing was very clear that she had not been thinking of only her ugliness and richness but was trying to visualize the problem in a general context. She had taken all the women in her purview. I knew that it is the theory of *Karma: Sanchit* (collected); *Prārabdha* (effective in the present) and *Āgāmi* (to be performed in the future). I said in my usual loud voice so that others also may hear me clearly:

"O Mahārāni Mallikā! Some women are irritable, susceptible to ire or anger. They are irate. If she is disobeyed or criticized even slightly, she is highly upset and extremely angry. She hears no argument as she is stubborn. At every opportune or inopportune moment she displays great resentment, punishing hatred and uncontrollable anger. She behaves accordingly. She does not believe in tenderness, sympathy, compassion, charity, donation and welfare of other living beings. She won't give essentials like food, drink, clothing, bedding, housing or luxuries like vehicles, unguents, scents or garlands to the needy, poor or Brāhmins, monks or ascetics. She is the jealous kind; deeply envious of prosperity, wealth, power, respect, homage or pleasure to others. When such a lady passes away; leaves this body and abode; and takes re-birth she is ill-formed, ugly and also poor. She is definitely a destitute with little or no wealth: neither of physique nor of mind; neither material nor spiritual, neither power nor influence."

"O Shākya Muni! As I'm ugly then I must have had uncontrollable anger and must have displayed great resentment in my previous birth."

"O Mahārāni Mallikā! Don't hurriedly arrive at a conclusion. Conclusions can be drawn when the answer to all the four questions are before us. First listen to the answers. Though, you are sitting idle and steady, your mind is active and looking at and running to many things."

"O Shākya Muni! I have been worrying too much for quite a long time. I have tried my level best to get a satisfactory answer. I have talked to many pundits, *jyotishies*, wise and learned ascetics but to no avail. I have been sceptical of my own thinking and behaviour. So, please forgive me and proceed. I have the patience to listen and a mind to retain the details."

"O Mahārāni Mallikā! Some women are irritable, susceptible to ire or anger. They are irate. If they are disobeyed or criticized even slightly, they are highly upset and extremely angry. They accept no argument as they are headstrong. At every opportune or inopportune moment they display great resentment, punishing hatred and uncontrollable anger. They behave accordingly. But they have tender feelings; are sympathetic and compassionate; have charitable nature; believe in donations and welfare of other living beings. They give essentials like food, drink, clothing, bedding, housing or luxuries like vehicles, unguents, scents or garlands to the needy, poor or Brāhmins, monks or ascetics.

So, when such a lady passes away; leaves this body and abode; and takes re-birth she is ill-formed, ugly but she possesses great wealth: finds all luxuries around her and exerts great influence on the persons close by and the events that are in any way related to her.

"O Mahārāni Mallikā! Some women are not irritable, not susceptible to ire or anger. They are not stubborn, never irate. If they are disobeyed or criticized even in their presence, they show no anger. They never lose their temper. But they are envious and jealous, deeply envious of prosperity, wealth, power, respect, homage or pleasure to others. When such a lady passes away; leaves this body and abode; and takes re-birth, wherever she is re-born, she is extremely beautiful, attractive, rather enchanting and graceful but she is poor with little wealth and virtually no influence. She is definitely a destitute."

I stopped for a few moments. I had tender feelings for the ugly queen who did not know what to do and how to get rid of her blemishes. Her garments told some tales of different notes but the scars narrated different stories. I was conscious of the changes on the face of Mallikā. They projected opposite feelings of increasing consternation and ease. I knew it would hurt her feelings but it was the most effective way. Truth is more powerful than anything else. I had to finish the answer. I finished it, raising my voice a bit more:

"O Mahārāni Mallikā! Some women are not irritable, not susceptible to ire or anger. They are not stubborn and never irate. They are disobeyed or criticized even in their presence, they show no anger. They never lose their temper. They have no envy, no jealousy. They are filled with pleasure at the prosperity, respect and worship of others. At the same time, they have tender feelings, sympathetic, compassionate; have a charitable nature; believe in donations and welfare of other living beings. They give essentials like food, drink, clothing, bedding, housing or luxurious like vehicles, unguents, scents or garlands to the needy, poor or Brāhmins, monks or ascetics. When such a lady passes away; leaves this body and abode; and takes re-birth, wherever she is re-born, she is extremely beautiful, attractive, rather enchanting and graceful. She is also rich. She possesses great wealth: finds all luxuries around her and exerts great influence on the persons close by and the events that are in any way related to her.

"O Mahārāni Mallikā! This is the cause and reason that some women in this world are ill-formed, ugly and also poor, destitute with little or no wealth.

This is the cause and reason that some women in this world are ill-formed, ugly but rich. They get great wealth and enjoy great prosperity and influence.

This is the cause and reason that some women in this world are extremely beautiful, attractive, rather enchanting and graceful but poor, destitute with little or no wealth.

This is the cause and reason that some women in this world are extremely beautiful, attractive, rather enchanting and graceful, and also rich. They enjoy immense wealth and great prosperity and influence."

I was silent. She waited for me to speak more or else she was collecting her own ideas or was measuring her own determination and metamorphosis as she did not look the same. She was a changed woman. There was neither fatigue nor anxiety, neither restlessness nor ego. There was satisfaction and peace on her face. She looked towards her maids lovingly, touching them with her eyes as a mother looks on her children. Then, she spoke in a sonorous, living voice:

"O Shākya Muni! O Blessed One! Now I know that in some earlier birth I was irritable, susceptible to ire and anger. I was irate and revengeful. I suppose that when I was opposed or disobeyed even slightly or criticized even slightly, I was highly upset and extremely angry. I displayed great resentment, punished people because of my uncontrollable anger. I accept it truthfully that because of that I'm ugly and ill-formed, full of blemishes and scars.

"O Blessed One! I believe that in some earlier birth I had tender feelings. I was sympathetic, compassionate; possessed charitable nature; believed in donations and welfare of other living beings. I gave away food, drink, clothing, bedding, housing or luxuries like vehicles, unguents, scents or garlands to the needy, poor or Brāhmins, monks or ascetics. I'm sure, because of that I'm rich, have wealth, power, influence and am obeyed.

"O Blessed One! For my future births, what have I to do? I know them now. I will have to win over my anger and throw it to dust. I will not be angry, jealous or envious of others. Anger and envy are not suited to a human heart. It turns it into inhuman. From now on, I will mend my ways and words. I will not order the maids who are from noble, brāhmin and householder families. I will give food and clothing and also respect and fragrance to the poor, the needy, monks, ascetics and Brāhmins.

"O Blessed One! I promise! I promise to you to be always good and compassionate to all. Now, I pray thee to accept me as a lay follower."

Voices from all sides repeated her words: 'I pray thee to accept me as a lay follower!' Saying so, she prostrated before me. With her a multitude prostrated. There was not a single person around me sitting or standing. I uttered:

"O Mahārāni Mallikā! You are free. You can take your own decision. You have to know and feel the changes and act accordingly. The option lies with you. O Good Fellows! You are free to take your decision and further steps. Do as you please! I accept!"

"O Blessed One! I see the truth. I know the fault. I will mend it. Before thee, before the presence of thousands of pious people, I declare that I enter Dharma to obey the Sangh and to be with the Buddha! So it be understood and accepted!

Dhammam Sharanam Swikāromi!
Sangham Sharanam Swikāromi!"

She lifted her head up confidently and with that all the heads came up. They all stood before me. No one was sitting. I had no idea how many men and women had come with Mallikā and how many among them entered the Sangh with her. They were huge in number. There were no rituals but the act of accepting them into Sangh and Dhamma was duly completed.

Ānand manages everything well. Monks are experts. They know what to do, how to do and when to do. They did everything meticulously. There was pleasure all around and the solemn chanting of:

Buddham Sharanam Gachhāmi!
Dhammam Sharanam Gachhāmi!
Sangham Sharanam Gachhāmi!

BUDDHA CLARIFIES KAMMA

Yesterday, I came here. It was *Chaturdashi*, the 14th day of the fortnight. It is *Purnimā* today. The full moon came out about an hour ago. I have been watching red area in the east that whitened and the upper part of moon was sighted. It grew larger and larger. The sky brightened. The tall trees caught the moon rays first. Then moonshine started falling on the huts and lands. The crops got a shiny bath, a cosmic one. I did not see but I knew it was on me as I saw the sun's light reflected through the moon on the places and persons. The sunshine and the moonlight cover all without discrimination. One increases energy, the other soothes the nerves, although it is one and the same. Sunshine emits energy, moonshine helps to absorb and store it. Through which it comes makes the difference. How and how much it is absorbed makes the difference. How and how much it is used and utilized makes the difference. If it is used for good deeds and for fostering care, it is a gain. If it is polluted and wasted, it is a loss. The loss of anything raises doubts about our ability; the loss of energy raises question on our existence. The use and the quality of use depend on the knowledge, culture, refinement and inner light of an individual and of society.

One after another, all the monks have gathered in front and the sides. Today, there is no one at the back. Only a few householders are present and some others are coming. It is a pleasure to find people engrossed in discourses but it is a pleasure of the highest order to see people following the teachings to the best of their ability and ingenuity, and making their lives better and better. The seed that is sown, sprouted, yielded saplings, grew, branched, matured, bloomed and bore fruits: healthy, sweet and fragrant.

The struggle of the seed begins much before its birth and continues even after its death. The youth feel that they have not as yet begun their struggle, the struggle lies ahead; the old feel that they have lost their struggle. It has resulted in their defeat. No, no! The struggle continues. It is not the wrestling of two persons or states; it is the struggle for completing a life; for fulfilling the needs with deeds for physical health and mental satisfaction; for worldly pleasures and spiritual happiness in the world with the family; carrying the load. The load is not a burden. They are aggrieved that feel the responsibilities to be burden. No, the responsibilities are there for a person to act; not to react. Act with the best of your ability, skill and that is all. Idleness kills. Misdeeds destroy. Reactions pinch. Burden pricks. Work reduces tension and depression. Work and be relaxed. Sit idle and feel the prick. Action gives pleasure. Others in action give pleasure. Watch others working and it is pleasure. Life is like that: very beautiful, and full of energy and power. It can well be the energy of body and mind and the power of knowledge and wisdom.

Wrinkles show and represent the energy, power, knowledge and wisdom as well as action, so do deeds, both good deeds and misdeeds. It is all written in the natural language of wrinkles. Wrinkles are powerful tales. They don't show failure or prosperity but struggle and action. They are the remains of dreams: meaningful, powerful and special. Face reading is fascinating and wrinkled figures are respectable. Respect their past to derive inspiration for the remaining actions and be engaged in future: near future and distant future. Ah! It is all *Kamma*! Oh! It is all *Kamma*! Bravo! It is all *Kamma*.

I was engrossed both in the beauty of Nature and the *Kamma* of human beings which had originated from the incessant *Kamma* by Nature. A monk slowly came to me and said:

"O Enlightened One! On behalf of all present here, I request you, please deliver a discourse!"

I turned my head and whispered: "Oh Yes!" I sat up, surveyed the crowd, looked up towards the moon and the colourful nature then turned towards the monks who were sitting there in large number. I gave a cursory glance towards the people who were coming and taking a seat. I took my favourite lotus posture and started delivering the sermon.

"O Monks! After I realized the truth, I declared four kinds of Kamma. Today, I shall analyse and explain them.

There are four kinds of *Kamma*. There are:

1st Dark Kamma with dark results;

2nd Bright Kamma with bright results;

3rd Dark and Bright Kamma with dark and bright results; and

4th Kammas that are neither Dark nor Bright receives with neither dark nor bright results.

It is the *Kamma* (Karma or deeds), which determines peace, pleasure and prosperity in life or poverty, pain or regress or a balanced or imbalanced mixture of the two. Good Karmas lead to good and happy results while bad karmas result in pain and suffering. The correct guidance is required so that the lay mass can know their moral, ethical and pure karmas. One can guide others regarding *Kamma* in various ways, provided that one performs only bright deeds and feels the bad effects of dark deeds. People with refined nature are the best guides. One can also learn and be wise through association with superior persons, listening to the good *Dhamma*, proper attention and practice in accordance with *Dhamma*. Pure and meritorious *Kamma* needs a lot of refinement. It must be understood by all.

If not, then they can act in darkness and perform dark deeds. Because of their ignorance, they may face dark results. Now the question is: what is dark *Kamma* with dark results? Dark deeds can be performed by body, mind or speech. Any act that inflicts injury to other living being in any form through body, speech or mind will be dark *Kamma*. Whosoever inflicts injury and gives pain after death takes birth in a darker hell-like zone and undergoes the experiences and pains of hell. He does afflictive volitional deeds and is reborn in afflictive world and lives in afflictive contacts. That life is extremely painful. These are dark deeds and their dark results.

Now, what are bright *Kamma* with bright results? The good, pure and meritorious deeds with body, mind or speech that help others lead a healthy and happy life are bright deeds. The person who has no afflictive volitional formation of mind, speech or body, performs such un-afflictive deeds and after death is reborn in an un-afflictive world where he lives in prosperity and health with pleasure. That life is extremely joyful and pleasant. He feels elated and receives honour and respect. That is the bright result of bright deeds.

Now, what are dark and bright *Kamma* with dark and bright results. It is the general practice of the common people. They do some good and some bad deeds. They hardly distinguish and discriminate between them. They work out of lust and for immediate gains. What we get by wrong means and misconduct, we lose easily and quickly and the net saving is in the negative. Those are the people that generate both an afflicted volitional formation of body, mind and speech and un-afflicted volitional formations of body, mind and speech. Because of such mixed deeds, after death they are reborn in the world that is pleasant and painful, afflicted and un-afflicted. Living in that mixed condition those persons experience a mixture of pleasure and pain. This is called dark and bright *Kamma* with dark and bright results.

Now, what are the *Kammas* that are neither dark nor bright that give neither dark nor bright results? In fact, such *Kammas* lead to the destruction of *Kamma*. 'The volition to abandon the dark *Kamma* with dark results, and to abandon bright *Kammas* with bright results, and to abandon the dark and bright *Kamma* with dark and bright results – this is called the *Kamma* that is neither dark nor bright, with neither dark nor bright results, which leads to the destruction of *Kamma*.

Volitional formations bring about rebirth into an appropriate world. It is clear that the world in which we are born, and the quality of our experience in this world, reflect the nature and extent of our conduct and actions in the previous life.

It is the conduct that is important and also the spirit behind the conduct. It is clear that we are responsible for our good or bad actions and heirs to their *Karmic* consequences, whether favourable or unfavourable. No exaggerated importance should be attached to anything else. It makes no difference whether the doer was a seer or an ignorant person. One has to face the results of his deeds and conduct. In place of thinking about an infinite number of combinations, one must concentrate on bright deeds for bright results and avoid to the best of one's ability the dark deeds to avoid darker results."

I stopped speaking and changed my posture. I changed to another favourite posture, the reclining one. The monks and the laymen paid homage and started returning. I closed my eyes to give them relief.

BUDDHA REITERATES THE KNOWN TRUTH

One day, when the monks and others were seated, Ānand came to me and said: "O the Enlightened One! Please guide us on what we should contemplate?"

I accepted by only moving my head in the affirmative. I looked at the faces of all sitting there in expectation. I assumed the lotus posture and began the discourse in contemplative mood and thoughtful words:

"O Monks! All human beings have a tendency to ignore the perennial truth. They feel that they can win over them by ignoring them. Many men hold the idea that they can search out ways and means to alter the absolute truth. The absolute truth cannot be altered and if it is altered, then it is not the absolute truth. People in the past have tried to win or alter it, but in vain. Even at present, some believe they can avoid the truth and are busy in searching some means to win over the truth.

O Monks! What are those known truths that are absolute and perennial? They are:

Everyone is sure to become old. None can avoid ageing.

Everyone is sure to become ill. None can avoid illness.

Everyone is sure to die. None can avoid death.

Everyone must part with and must be separated from whatever is dear and beloved to him or her. None can avoid final separation from everything that one possesses and loves and saves.

Everyone is the owner of his or her actions, owns the actions, heir to those actions. From actions they have sprung, their birth has been caused by their actions, are deeply related to their actions. They have performed them, have been protected by them, have safeguarded them and hence are liable for each and every action of theirs. They know it that whatever actions they have been performing: good or bad, full of jealousy or compassion, charitable or lustful, they own them. None can disown one's actions.

O Monks! There are many good reasons that a man or a woman, a householder or monk, must contemplate that they are sure to become old and cannot avoid ageing. What will they have in their store of action during their old age when they are unable to function a lot because of old age weaknesses? During their youthful days, people take pride in their youth. They feel infatuated with youthfulness and lead an evil life in deeds, words or thoughts or all the three. But one who often contemplates the certainty of old age, will not be led to evil deeds by the pride of youth. The pride will either vanish or weaken. For that one important reason, one should think about the certainty of old age.

O Monks! There are many good reasons that a man or a woman, a householder or monk, must contemplate that they are sure to become ill. None can avoid illness. When they were healthy and powerful they had the pride in their health and felt infatuated by the pride of health; and infatuated with health they led an evil life in deeds, words or thoughts or all the three. But one who often contemplates the certainty of illness, his or her pride will either vanish or weaken. For that one important reason, one should think about the illness.

O Monks! There are many good reasons that a man or a woman, a householder or monk, must contemplate that it is certain that everyone must part with and must be separated from whatever is dear and beloved to him or her. None can avoid the final separation from everything that one possesses, loves and saves. People are full of lustful desires for accumulating wealth and luxurious things for their dear and beloved ones. They feel inflamed with those desires and lead an evil life in deeds, words or thoughts or all the three. But one who often contemplates about the separation from his or her near and dear ones, his or her desires and acts either vanish or weaken. For that very reason, one should often contemplate over separation from near and dear ones.

So, O Monks! There are many good reasons that a man or a woman, a householder or monk, must contemplate that it is certain that everyone is the owner of his or her actions, owns the actions and is the heir to those actions. From actions they have sprung, their birth has been caused by their actions, and they are deeply related to their actions. They have performed them, have been by protected by them, have safeguarded them and hence are liable for each and every action of theirs. They know it that whatever actions they have been performing: good or bad, full of jealousy or compassion, charitable or lustful, they own them. None can disown one's actions. There are numerous human beings that lead an evil life in deeds, words or thoughts or all the three. But one who often contemplates about the responsibility of all his or her good deeds and misdeeds either does no misdeeds, or those misdeeds are reduced drastically in quantity and quality.

So, O Monks! Everyone should think and contemplate like this: 'I'm not the only one who is sure to become old; sure to fall ill; and sure to die or to be separated from all others; and responsible for my deeds. All who take birth, come to the world and pass away; and are reborn, they are subject to age, illness, death and separation; and are responsible for all actions and will get punishment or reward accordingly.'

Such persons attain light. They make progress. They mend their habits, thinking and deeds. They become cultured and refined. They think of own interest and the interests of that of other human and non-human beings. They see and pursue the right path. It is *Dhammam Nirupam*, looking at the religion. They feel the goal to be near and proceed on that path with zeal and enthusiasm.

Eventually, they get *nibbāna*, freedom from the cycle of birth and rebirth and worldly pain and suffering.

You must contemplate like that and spread such contemplation to enable lay men to feel the reality, know truth, see the path and pursue *nibbāna.*

May everyone be healthy and think healthy!"

I stopped speaking but my thinking continued. It usually happens that I keep on thinking after the discourses are over. Actually my inner discourse is never over. It continues. Thinking continues. Ideas pour in and are poured out; yet they grow. They have been growing and continue to grow.

It grows with *sati*, mindfulness; with *Dhamma vichāra*, investigation; *vīrya*, energy; *passachi*, relaxation; *samādhi*, concentration and *uppekkhā*, equanimity.

But it will reduce drastically if one keeps *kāmachhanda,* lustful desires; *vyāpāda*, ill-will, hatred and anger; *thina meddhā*, torpor and languor; *uddachcha kukkuchhā*, restlessness and worries and *vilikichchā*, sceptical doubts.

I know, thinking in the right direction will make one do only good and meritorious deeds. A person with a clear and pure mind and conscience can never be evil or do evil.

As only the human species have special powers of accomplishment so our life is precious. Because our life is precious, our deeds must be pious. We must keep our body clean, our enjoyments ethical and the deeds virtuous. All our pious deeds must be dedicated or must be for the general benefit of both the sentient and non-sentient beings.

The real strength of human beings lies in *vivek-gyān*, the discrimination between the good and bad. For sustaining through life material accumulation is needed, and for health, happiness and continued existence that accumulation must be through moral and ethical means. If it is otherwise, then pain and suffering in different forms will increase and life will be like living in a lower hell. If there is no generosity and charity then the fall is definite. Accumulation is alright but there should not be attachment to accumulation. All these things can be done while living among the multitude and by fulfilling all the social and moral responsibilities. They get salvation and freedom from the cycle easily who lead a moral and ethical life by doing meritorious works and wholesome deeds. It is non-attachment and renunciation that matters at every step. Renunciation does not mean leaving the society and casting aside all the responsibility; one can leave society for acquiring better and higher knowledge but one must use that wisdom for the betterment of life; and one must fulfill the responsibility. An irresponsible life is no life at all. I too left home but I have undertaken a greater and higher responsibility than looking after the usual and daily chores of a kingdom. I did not leave home for my personal gain or accumulation of material wealth. I left my palace and ensured my renunciation by only partially announcing it, rather unannounced, for the benefit of all; for searching a way out for the cessation of general pain and the suffering of all; for acquiring higher wisdom and for sharing it with others. It was ordained. I had to do it. I am doing it and I will keep on doing it till I feel fit to do it. I have taken that general moral, pious and religious responsibility by and upon myself.

BUDDHA TEACHES MONKS

One day, when I was staying at Tikandaki Grove, near Sāket, a Monk came to me with a request. After paying homage he said:

"O Blessed One! Please teach us in the discourse today, what is living by the Dhamma? In what way do monks live by the Dhamma? Who else live by the Dhamma?"

I nodded my head in acceptance and sat up. I took water from the vessel and took my favourite lotus posture. I was ready for a long discourse. I surveyed the monks and the mass and began my speech:

"O Monks! Listen with intent and discrimination! A monk masters all the nine aspects of Dhamma: 1st the discourses; 2nd the mixed prose; 3rd expositions; 4th Verses; 5th Inspired Utterances; 6th Brief Sayings; 7th Birth Stories; 8th Marvellous Accounts and 9th Miscellanies. He passes his days and years, engaged in that mastery of the outer garb of the Dhamma and misses the real aspect. He neglects seclusion, meditation and application of all those things in life and conduct. He does not apply himself to internal tranquility of mind. He fails to apply his wisdom and understand its meaning. He fails to follow them in his life. He is a monk who is engrossed and engaged in the learning and mastery of Dhamma; he is not living by Dhamma.

O Monks! A monk teaches the Dhamma in minute details to others as he learns and masters it. He passes his days and years, engaged in that mastery of the outer garb of the Dhamma and teaching it. In that process he misses the real aspect. He neglects seclusion, meditation and application of all those things in life and conduct. He does not follow the teachings and lessons in life. He does not apply himself to internal tranquility of mind. He fails to apply his wisdom and understand its meaning. He is a monk who is engrossed and engaged in the mastery and teaching of Dhamma; he is not living by Dhamma.

O Monks! A monk recites the Dhamma correctly and in rhythmical tone to others as he learns and masters it. He passes his days and years, engaged in that mastery of the outer garb of the Dhamma and in the recitation. In that prolonged engagement he misses the real aspect. He neglects seclusion, meditation and application of all those things in life and conduct. He does not follow the teachings and lessons in life. He does not apply himself to internal tranquility of the mind. He fails to apply his wisdom and understand its meaning. He is a monk who is engrossed and engaged in the mastery and teaching of Dhamma; he is not living by Dhamma.

O Monks! A monk ponders over, examines in detail and mentally investigates the Dhamma and discusses it with others as he had learnt and mastered it. He passes his days and years, engaged in such examination and analysis of the outer garb of the Dhamma and misses the real aspect. He neglects seclusion, meditation and application of all those things in life and conduct. He does not follow the teachings and lessons in life. He does not apply himself to internal tranquility of mind. He fails to apply his wisdom and understand its meaning. He is a monk who is engrossed and engaged in the mastery and teaching of Dhamma; he is not living by Dhamma.

O Monks! A monk reads, listens to and learns and masters the discourses, mixed prose, expositions, verses, inspired utterances, birth stories and other accounts. He passes his days and years not engaged in mastery of the outer garb of the Dhamma but thinks of the real aspect. He never neglects seclusion. He meditates on and applies all those teachings in life and conduct. He follows the words and lessons in life. He applies himself to internal tranquility of mind understanding its meaning. He is a monk who lives the ideas expressed in Dhamma. He is the monk who lives by Dhamma.

Studying and learning Dhamma and its scriptures is one thing; teaching Dhamma is another thing; recitation of the dhamma scriptures is yet another thing; analysis and examination is also definitely different but reflection as aids to personal spiritual development is quite a different thing. If these are ends in themselves then they are not living by Dhamma but **if they are used as methods of self cultivation and internal progress towards Arhantship then it is living by Dhamma**.

Knowing moral codes is one thing and obeying the moral dictates and doing everything accordingly is another thing. The doing gives meaning to deeds and life. Knowing is lifeless if not lived accordingly. Teaching religion is one thing and following religiosity in life, conduct and deeds is another thing. Following Dhamma in thought, word and deeds gives meaning. Mere teaching is lifeless if if religious dictums are not followed in words and deeds. Recitation of the Dhamma scriptures is one thing and leading a life in accordance with Dhamma scriptures is another thing. Leading a life in thought, words and deeds according to the recited words gives meaning. Mere recitation is lifeless, if life is not led according to the ideas expressed in them. It must be applied for inner purity and ample growth."

Ten Noble Abodes

Once I was dwelling at Kammāsa Damma, a town of the Kurus. There was a very big congregation of monks. On their request, I delivered a discourse in which I explained the Ten Noble Abodes. I said:

"O Monks! There are ten abodes where the noble ones have abided in the past; where they abide in the present and where they will reside in the future.

The ten abodes are :

- A monk has abandoned five factors.
- A monk possesses six factors.
- A monk has a single guard.
- A monk has fourfold support.
- A monk has driven away many separate truths.
- A monk has given up seeking.
- A monk has clarified his thoughts.
- A monk has calmed the bodily formation.
- A monk has become well liberated in mind.
- A monk has become well liberated by wisdom.

How has a monk abandoned five factors? The monk who has driven off and abandoned a) sensual desire; b) ill will; c) sloth and torpor; d) restlessness and worry; and e) doubts; has abandoned five factors.

How does a monk possess six factors? Having seen directly a form through eyes when a monk is neither elated nor dejected; he dwells in equanimity and mindfulness; and has clear comprehension, then he possesses a factor. When a monk hears a sound with the ear, smells an odour with the nose, tastes something with the tongue, contacts an object with the body or recognizes a mind-object with the mind yet he is neither elated nor dejected; has clear comprehension and dwells in equanimity and mindfulness; then the monk possesses six factors.

How has a monk a single guard? When the mind of a monk is well guarded by mindfulness then he has a single guard.

How has a monk fourfold support? When a monk uses something after adequate reflection; endures something after correct thinking; avoids something after due deliberations; and dispels something after taking different things into consideration, then the monk has fourfold support.

How has a monk driven away many separate truths? There are many separate truths held by seekers, ascetics, and Brāhmins such as:

The world is eternal or the world is not eternal.

The world is finite or the world is infinite.

The soul is one thing and the body is another or the soul and body are the same.

The Tathāgata does not exist after death or the Tathāgata both exists and does not exist after death.

If and when a monk has discarded all such notions, driven them away, renounced and rejected them, and abandoned and relinquished them, then the monk has driven away many separate truths.

How has a monk given up seeking? A monk has abandoned the search for sensual pleasure and the search for becoming and has suspended the search for a holy life, then the monk has given up seeking.

How has a monk clarified his thoughts? When a monk has abandoned sensual thoughts, thoughts of ill will and thoughts of violence, then the monk has clarified his thoughts.

How has a monk calmed the bodily formation? With the abandoning of pleasure and pain; and with the previous passing away of joy and sadness; when a monk enters and dwells in the fourth state of *gyāna,* which is neither painful nor pleasant and includes the purification of mindfulness by equanimity; then the monk has calmed down the bodily formation.

How has a monk become well liberated in mind? When a monk's mind is liberated from lust, hatred and delusion then the monk is well liberated in mind.

How has a monk become well liberated by wisdom? When a monk understands well that lust, hatred, anger and delusion have been completely abandoned by him and cuts off the root, making it barren like a palm-tree-stumps; and has obliterated other traits that they are no more subject to rise again in future; then that monk is well liberated by wisdom.

O Monks! Then it is very clear that whosoever noble one in the past abided in noble abodes, he abided or they all abided in just these ten noble abodes.

O Monks! Whosoever noble one in the present abides in noble abodes he abides or they all abide in only these ten noble abodes.

O Monks! Whosoever noble one in the future will abide in noble abodes he will or they all will abide in only these ten noble abodes."

Six Disrespectful Abodes

"O Monks! There are six disrespectful abodes. They are:

1. Anger and revenge;
2. Contemptuous and domineering;
3. Envious and avaricious;
4. Deceitful and fraudulent;
5. Evil wishes and wrong views;
6. Holding own views tenaciously.

Those that have such vile and despicable nature and character dwell in disrespectful abodes. They have no deference towards me, the Dhamma and the Sangha. Such a monk has neither obtained the training correctly nor has cleaned himself. Such monks create dispute in the Sangha and bring disrespect, which harms every effort and the cause and aim of teachings. It is unhappiness and loss for the mass, the multitude, the people, human beings and other beings at large; and harm and suffering for them.

O Monks! If you see and find these roots of disputes either in yourselves or externally in others; try with all your might to erase and abandon them from the roots; and ensure that such roots do not appear again or resurface.

O Monks! Think of it deeply! Think over it deeply! What is essential: only mastery over learning; only the teaching of Dhamma; only the analysis and examination of Dhamma or applying the teachings in life; or to follow the marvels in conduct and deeds; to get internal tranquility; and thus to become an Arhant? Remember that the aim of Dhamma is Nibbāna and not its simple study. Know the Dhamma to use its teachings! Know the teachings to live accordingly! Introspect and follow! Acquire Arhantship and freedom from the cycle of birth and rebirth!

Sabbe Santu Nirāmayāh!"

I stopped speaking and arose. Slowly, I proceeded towards the fragrant flowers. Their fragrance was beckoning I had to meet them, look at them and listen to them. With the blow of a light wind, their mixed smell increased and came gushing to welcome me.

BUDDHA SHOWS NO ANGER

Whenever I'm physically idle, reclining or taking rest, my ideas get concentrated and mind works in a creative manner. Either I recall something that I have already discussed in some discourse or I take something new to ponder over. Today, Mahāgovind is coming again and again to mind. It is a story of the past that I had once narrated. In it, I had compared this lovely and loving country, the most ancient one and of course, the most cultured one; to a cart. I had divided it in seven provinces: 1st Kalinga; 2nd Potana; 3rd Avanti; 4th Sauvira; 5th Videha; 6th Anga and 7th Kāsi. It is a great nation with balance and variety. It has very high hills and very low lands and deep seas and great and fertile places in between. Travelling mostly on foot, I have lived with Nature and enjoyed its colour and fragrance; sweet juicy fruit and a wide variety of grains. I cannot count how many places are dear to me.

My mind returns often to that richness. I like and appreciate such mindfulness. I have discussed and exhaustively explained the path of mindfulness in the Mahāsatipatthanā Sutta. It consists in keeping the mind (*sati)* alert *(upatthana)* to what is happening inside one's mind; inside the mind and all around. It is deep consciousness: to be conscious of each little and wild sound and each light and heavy movement. Even when one's eyes are closed the flickering movement be caught and the things that are happening can be known. It can be done only when the mind is really alert and conscious.

Ahā! The Lakkhana Suttanta! It always remains alive in my mind! In it, I have discussed in detail, the act by which a person acquires the 32 signs of great men. Nothing more is needed when those signs and qualities are acquired!

At this particular hour the Singalovāda Suttanta is also coming to mind. It balances all for it is for the benefit of the lay devotees. It is a comprehensive discourse for them. They must be taken care of. They need the guidance more and more at almost every step as they are more ignorant than others, particularly the monks. I'm sure this *Suttanta* will keep on guiding the people in the near future and even in the very remote future. It will change the life for better refinement and greater spiritual gain. It will be the basis of the common people, the lay devotees. They will be able to see the path and move fearlessly on it with faith, hope and confidence. I'm sure it will be repeated infinite times for millennia to come, for crores of years. It will take off *avidyā*, ignorance and establish *sheela*, good conduct among the good as well as the downtrodden; among those who are on the right path of righteousness and also among those that have lost their path; and are moving in wilderness.

Most men are neither attached nor detached. On the contrary I am attached to all and detached from all. I have affection for each one but I am not emotionally attached to anyone. I love all, I am aggrieved for all and I respect all. It may seem to be paradox but it is not. I balance the opposites. Balance is there at the centre of the opposites. It is love and respect that endures pains and sufferings. I am far away from my parents but I love and respect them. I am far away from Yashodharā and Rāhul yet I love and respect them. I love all the places, plants, trees, birds, animals, insects and respect them. They are all dear to me. I have a lot of affinity for them.

I am away from my palace so that I can be among many and do something concrete and creative for all. If all are well, I am well. If all are ill, I cannot be healthy. I may return but won't stay there as I have no longing and deep emotional attachment. I am for them as I am for others. They are not only part of my ideas and thinking, but also a part of my being. All beings are in my being. I do not need to tell anyone. They know it. They will know it. They have accepted. They will accept. I have accepted. I am accepted. Acceptance is positive. I deny none. Denial is negative. Denial is painful, deathlike. Acceptance is pleasant and life-like.

People have misconceptions. They think of only themselves and their very close ones. They have a wrong notion that if they are healthy and happy then it is all. But they forget that they can never be happy if others are suffering. Who will plough their fields? Who will harvest their products? Who will load the carts and bring the produce home? Who will make houses for them? Who will weave and stitch clothes for them?

Oh! No, no! One is dependent on many. One's health and happiness is not sustainable. It can never be. One family alone cannot be healthy and happy. We are dependent on many families. If one family is confined to itself then it will not get help from others. How can the kings and rich merchants live if they have no workers, no soldiers; none to look after what they possess.

Who will fight alone with the storms and tempests? Who will stand alone against floods and deluges? Who will face the diseases and dacoits alone? Survival depends on interdependence. One must think of others.

One must plough the fields of hearts and minds; sow the seeds of love, faith and hope and harvest the crops of compassion, kindness and charity. I acquired the light and the truth. Enlightenment dawned, wisdom came. I am also a farmer. My ploughs, spades, sickles and axes are different; different are the seeds, flowers and fruits. The flowers of good deeds are different. The scented smell of natural flowers goes only with the wind, but the smell of good deeds, good character and fragrance of good moral intent goes even against the wind.

To survive and to be healthy and happy, one must avoid the extremes and achieve a balance among humans; among other creatures; among deeds and also among emotions.

But there are numerous persons who are always at the extreme. They have extreme fear and extreme anger. I remember the Shrota-āpanna Brāhmni, the wife of a Brāhmin who had reached the state of Arhantship, kept me always in memory and chanted my Mantra: 'I salute that God, the Arhat Samyak-sambuddha!' I learnt the details of her story after I had faced the anger of at least two brothers. Later on, I had to face the other two brothers. I liked them. They had good knowledge but no practical wisdom and had not followed the knowledge that they had acquired by reading and memorizing. A man who reads much good literature but never tries to bring it into practice is like that cowherd who counts the number of cows every day before taking them for grazing and also after returning from the pasture, but has no proprietary right over any of them. He simply looks after them. The Brāhmins were only the guards of the knowledge that they had. They never followed the dictates and hence they were far from being cultured and refined. They had all the worldly weaknesses: ego, pride, desires, attachments, jealousy and also anger and sense of revenge.

One day, she did chant 'I salute that God, the Arhat Samyak-sambuddha!' when she stumbled slightly while feeding some Brāhmins. Akkosha Bhārdwāja was angry. He said: 'This woman from the fallen community usually chants the name and praises that tonsured Shramana. O Shudrā! I will go now to that Shramana and discuss religion. I will see what and how far he has achieved. What knowledge does he possess? What greatness has he acquired?'

She said politely: 'You can do whatever you like but I don't know that there is any wiser person in the world who can defeat Shāstā in any debate regarding religion. Still, you should go and ask whatever doubts you have in mind. His answer will satisfy you.'

Akkoshaka Bhārdwāja came to me. He showed utmost discourtesy. There was no salutation and no exchange of greetings. The formalities were cast aside. Some persons never realize the value of folding hands and greeting the other. They wrongly feel that if they bow they may become degraded. It is not the gradation it is the human value and recognition of rare wisdom that human beings possess.

He stood before me in the most arrogant manner. He was expecting that I would show anger and he would get an opportunity to chide me. He had no idea that I had won over anger and jealousy long before I attained Buddhatva. He asked very rudely:

Kim su chhetvā sukham seti? Kim su chhetvā na sochati?
Kissassu eka dhammassa vadham rochesi, Gautamā?

'O Gautam! Tell me. After cutting and destroying what a man can sleep peacefully? After cutting and destroying what a man never feels aggrieved? What is that religion whose destruction has importance in your eyes?'

I wondered and smiled. The man knew the answer. It was his weakness. He had failed to destroy it. He knew it yet was asking me. With that broad smile on my lips I answered:

Krodham chhetvā sukham seti, krodham chhetvā na sochati;
Krodhassa visamulassa, madhuragassa Brāhmana;
Vadham ariyā pasan santi, tam hi chhetvā na sochati.

'Brāhmin! A man can cut and destroy anger and get sound sleep. After cutting, throwing out and destroying anger a man never feels aggrieved. It is the religion of anger that one can easily cut and destroy. The destruction of anger has importance in my eyes because the net result of anger is always painful. It is like poison. In some cases and in the beginning it may appear sweet but later on it gives a lot of pain and suffering. So, O Brāhmin! The wise feel no sadness after destroying anger.'

He immediately realized that I knew what he was thinking and also his greatest weakness. He sat down. He was thoughtful, calm and at ease. After a long silence he expressed his wish to accept Pravrajyā, renunciation. He became a monk.

This was not the end. It was the beginning. His younger brother, Ākroshaka Bhārdwāja was very angry to hear the news that his brother was so impressed by the Shākya Muni that he opted for renunciation and got initiated in Dhamma. In that great anger he came to the Venuvan to abuse me. I neither abuse nor accept abuses. They return to those that abuse. Without waiting for an enquiry he started hurling abuse and strong words against me in my presence. I smiled and retained the smile. He was tired of abusing but got no encouragement from any corner. There was none else to listen to him and I was simply smiling back. It was too much for his nerves. He slowed down, then stopped. I silently indicated a seat. He sat down. First I offered water. He was tired, thirsty and hungry. I signaled a monk to bring food for him. It was brought and courteously placed before him. Again, I quietly requested him to eat, which he did. He was given a bed to sleep.

After taking a long nap, he woke up. He was a changed man. He came directly to me, fell on my feet and started weeping. I stood up, helped him to get up and silently embraced him. He held me tightly and wept for quite a long time. I silently patted him and allowed him to wash off the moss from his mind and heart. He took time to be normal. The first thing that he uttered: 'O Shāstā! Make me your disciple. I have to learn a lot. I think I have no inner strength. Allow me to get initiated into the Dhamma.'

I said: 'O Brāhmin! You have a lot of courage and inner strength. You don't know it. It is flowing in wrong direction in negative thought and words. Use sweet words; think and do good for all and that is all. You will be initiated in the Dhamma right now.'

Bhārdwāja was initiated. I was only an onlooker. I was present there. But the expert and courteous monks did everything else.

Even this one was not the end of the episode. It started another event. The news of the renunciation and initiation of the Brāhmin reached his home land. His two younger brothers, Sundarika Bhārdwāja and Vilingaka Bhārdwāja were angry to learn about it. They could not control their anger. They sped towards the Venuvan to punish me. When they came before me they were burning with the heat of anger. I simply swallowed and digested their harsh abusive words. They were so angry that they were unable to think anything new and kept on repeating the same things again and again. My stable smile made them realize that they were saying nothing new. Suddenly, they were silent and remained silent for a long time.

Then they looked towards each other and fell at my feet, but I raised them and embraced them. They were like me: human and lively. They were ruled by the negative qualities. In that warm embrace they were throwing their anger and ego away. I had long ago thrown them off completely out of my nature.

All the four brothers were very sincere and intelligent. They followed the teachings and deed, only good deeds. It was a great concentrated effort on their part. Happily enough, all the four brothers achieved Arhanship and were liberated. It was a great and very happy ending to what seemed at first sight a very rough behaviour. It is not important from where we begin our journey. Where we end our journey is very important. It was all peace and freedom for them.

Once, there was a big congregation at Venuvan. Before I began the discourse, these four brothers were living brightly in my memory so, when I started the discourse I narrated the whole incident in detail and declared: 'O Monks! O Householders! I have immense peace inside so I never hate or feel anger for bad elements. It gives greater solace and tranquility.

'O Monks! O Householders!

Akkosam vadha bandham cha, aduttho yo titikkhati;
Khanti balam balānikam, tam aham brumi Brāhmanam.

The fact is that I accept him and declare him as Brāhmin who without making his mind dirty tolerates the harsh and abusive words of the notorious and bad persons; forgiveness is his power and peace is his fighting army.

Such a person is a Brāhmin who shows no anger or is not aggrieved at anything; who listens to and tolerates all the ten types of blame and abusive language. Since he possesses immense peace inside he uses it again and again with greater zeal and enthusiasm to defeat the very purpose of the bad people.

The effect of that discourse was so deep on the householders that many from among them opted for renunciation of all worldly possessions and initiation into Dhamma. They were amply rewarded when they concentrated on meritorious deeds and meditation.

Sabbe Shantu Shāntatā!"

BUDDHA ADVISES MONKS

Life is not only this or that. Life is mixed. Since it is mixed, it is complex. The nature and extent of its mix and complexity vary in degree both in quality and quantity. The mixing becomes more complex when we find the physical presence of an infinite number of living beings and non-living things, which are not exactly non-living, but whose life differs from those that move. So, it is better to think them to be non-moving in place of non-living. The complexity of life's mix grows when we find the presence of infinite number of ideas. The growing and maturing ideas change the uses of everything and everyone from place to place, from time to time and from season to season.

Man is one and yet is not one. Dhamma is one and yet is not one. An individual is one and yet is not one. A monk is one and yet a monk is not one: he is a beginner, a learner, a teacher, a preceptor, a guide, a follower and much more. It adds to the complexity. The stages of perception, growth, maturity and accomplishments are mixed and complex.

These ideas flashed in my mind as many other ideas have dawned upon me, when I saw the Venerable Ānand approaching towards me with many new monks when I was dwelling among the Magadhans at Andhakāvinda. Some senior monks also accompanied them. Other senior Monks were coming in another group along with Sāriputra. When they were seated after paying homage and salutation, I addressed Ānand, Sāriputra and the monks.

"O Venerable Ānand! O Venerable Sāriputra! O monks! Listen to me intently. It is particularly for the new monks but the senior monks must know them and remember to guide others and to ensure its implementation.

The monks who are newcomers, who have recently gone forth and have just come to this Dhamma and discipline, should be exhorted, settled and established at least in five things.

First, they should be virtuous and dwell restrained by the restraint of *Pātimokkha*. They should be perfect in conduct and resort and feel great danger in the slightest fault. First know the training rules and then train in them.

Second, they should guard the doors of sense faculties with mindfulness as the guard; with discerning mindfulness; with a well protected mind and with a maintaining mindfulness.

Third, they should not talk much; place limits on to their conversation and thus they should settle and be established in the limitation of talking.

Fourth, they should be forest dweller; in remote lodging far away from home mostly at lonely places, forests, gardens and woodlands. Thus, they should settle and be established in bodily withdrawal.

Fifth, they should possess the right view and see things in the right perspective and be established in it."

When I stopped for a few moments, I heard voices of acceptance from every corner. I have been always sure that my words are heard with due concentration and followed meticulously. They are repeated again and again by one disciple or the other; by monks or laymen. So they are always fresh in the mind and usually quoted at the right and most opportune moment. I found the time very ripe for teaching the monks and in the presence of the new disciples I repeated the teachings that I had given earlier on in Tikandaki Grove near Sāket regarding perceiving the repulsive in the un-repulsive and to abide from time to time perceiving un-repulsive in the repulsive; perceiving the repulsive from both the un-repulsive and repulsive as well as perceiving the un-repulsive from both repulsive and un-repulsive along with perceiving and abiding by equanimity, mindfulness and clear comprehension.

What the people don't easily realize is the fact that *kamma* is the field; consciousness is the seed and craving the moisture for the consciousness of the beings hindered by ignorance and fettered by craving to get established in a lower realm, intermediate realm or in the lofty realm. Due to the *kamma* there is a re-becoming in the future.

I discussed these and many more things before closing the discourse. This rare religious assembly of new and senior monks continued for a long time. All of them were serious, happy and satisfied. They requested and I declared the assembly to be over with the wish: *Gyānam Prāptavāna*!

In that grove I thought of Venuvan, an abode for the monks, and whenever Venuvan came to mind, the great king Bimbisār also comes alive talking in his idiosyncratic, confident and pleasant way. On my mental plate, I see him usually at two places: in the court sitting on the throne suggesting me to drop the idea of penance and to return home on the pretext of youthful age, which is not the right time to go for penance. I did not agree with him. Only during the youthful energetic days one can undertake hard, hot, rough and tough tasks. I went ahead, analyzed and synthesized and followed the wise advices. As a result, enlightenment dawned.

The second posture of the great king Bimbisār comes to my mind is that of the hills where I was staying after enlightenment. I had gone to his capital city to meet him. But the alert king knew everything. He came to meet me, nay, to me and to worship the enlightenment. He had brought many cartloads of gifts but the best gift was the Venuvan Vihar which he gifted as an abode of the monks. But first he and his courtiers and other men saluted me, some ladies performed *ārti*, obeisance with lighted lamps and incense sticks.

Then the king eulogized, praised me with different and heavy adjectives used mostly in the superlative degree, and heartily welcomed me and the monks. He promised to work for spreading the Dhamma, and afterwards he did it well. He made various arrangements that the work of Dhamma would continue even after his departure. That work is going on with all the dynamism and subtlety. I do remember that graceful appearance of the royalty.

Migāra and his mother Vishākhā also come to my mind. Vishākhā was not his mother. She was, in fact, his daughter-in-law. She knew me and had learnt of my teachings from childhood. When she was married to Migāra's son, the scenario at his place was not to her liking. They followed a path that she could not appreciate. She discussed my teachings with her father-in-law, Migāra. She suggested to him to listen to my discourses. He invited me and I stayed in his mansion. After listening to me he was metamorphosed and was really very grateful to his daughter-in-law, Vishākhā and one day, he announced 'Vishākhā has refined me and changed me so she is my spiritual mother.'

From there on he called her 'Mother'. That way Vishākhā became famous as Migāra's mother. People do not call her Vishākhā but the mother of Migāra.

Once, when I was dwelling in their mansion, many men and women accompanied by Migāra and Vishākhā came to me. They paid due respect and sat down around me. Vishākhā wished to know about the good qualities of women. I said:

"Vishākhā! A successful woman possesses four qualities. With those qualities she forges ahead towards victory. The qualities that a successful woman possesses are:

1. A woman is capable of doing and skilled in finishing her works;
2. She knows and diligently performs her husband's household chores;
3. She behaves in a way that is agreeable to her husband;
4. She safeguards the earnings of her husband.

A woman is capable of doing and skilled in finishing her works;

She knows and diligently performs her husband's household chores and manages the domestic help. She uses appropriate means; arranges everything properly and finishes her tasks well and in time. She gives adequate food to all who are dependent on her or her husband.

She behaves in a way that is agreeable to her husband. She will not commit a mistake. She never commits misdeeds or mischief towards her husband. She protects and safeguards the earnings of her husband.

Vishākhā! Listen to me carefully! But if such a successful woman is accomplished with faith in me; has virtue, generosity and wisdom and is free from misconduct, false speech, wine, liquor, and intoxicants; and if that woman is devoted to charity and has a noble and penetrative mind then that woman is free from disease, suffering, pain and lamentation. That woman forges ahead for victory in the spiritual world and lofty reālm."

FIVE DREAMS AS BODHISATTVA

When today, I sat here, my own dreams started coming to my mind, one by one in the beginning, then in a torrent. I'm sure my mind has stored all the dreams and has kept them alive. Since then, I have been thinking over those dreams: the soft, sweet and awesome phenomenon.

Dreams are meaningful. Dreams contain past happenings and also future events. Dreams are also related to expectations, desires, works, fears and suppressed feelings. It's a wonder that often dreams show very remote things, apparently having no relation to the present or future of the person or the relatives. In all its apparent and hidden details, dreams are meaningful.

But it is not easy to know their meaning because dreams are always and invariably in symbols. A subtle symbolic language is the specialty of every dream. Moreover, the symbols too are personal, closely knitted with the life and events of the person concerned. Yet the meaning can be crystal clear if it is analyzed with wisdom and insight; of course, by a person who has a tranquil mind, wisdom and insight and can concentrate on every aspect of a dream with ease and simplicity. Yet only the broader meaning can be given. The details cannot be given.

The most popular question related to dreams is that whether they came true or not. Dreams come true when such directives are consciously followed. When will the dream come true? It is almost impossible to give an exact time or even a close one.

If one does good and helps all who are around him or her; or come to him or her become good then the dreams will come true. Otherwise, it will be something non-existent. Dreams of both good and bad elements and also both good and bad dreams come true but good effects will depend on good deeds and the bad effects on misdeeds.

When the dreams are fresh then people are conscious whether it comes true or not. But slowly, dreams start losing importance and with the passage of time the dreams are forgotten and no one cares whether they came true or not. The reason behind is one's day-to-day busy schedule. All of us have tasks and are physically and mentally preoccupied everyday. Hence, it is but natural that they forget the dreams. Moreover, many people see many dreams. They can hardly keep track of those dreams since they have to keep many other things in mind and perform many other important tasks.

I too, do not keep track of my dreams but the dreams are alive in me. Some of the dreams that often return to my conscious mind are the dreams that I had before becoming the Tathāgata; the Arhant and Enlightened. I had five dreams when I was only a Bodhisattva.

What were they?

I dreamt that this mighty earth is my great bedstead; the mighty Himalayas, king of Mountains, are my pillow; my left hand rested on the Eastern Ghāt and the right hand on the Western Ghāt; both my feet were at the southern sea and my body had covered the whole of this vast land.

It meant that I would represent this vast land and this vast land would project me. I would know it and it would feel me. It ensured a new awakening unsurpassed; perfect assimilation of all its knowledge and thus total enlightenment, hitherto unseen and unfathomed. The future would gain and show complete control.

The second dream that I had was a lot different. I saw that from my navel sprouted and arose *tiriyā*, the sacred grass; and continued to grow until it touched the clouds.

This dream made it clear that I would know everything and every path from earth to heaven and would connect the earth and the sky. My knowledge would be based on the realities of the world but would have the power to change one into something spiritual and definitely cosmic; it would touch the sky. I would make new paths and show the existing ones.

In the third dream I saw, that white worms with black heads crawled on my legs up to the knees, and covered them.

This dream declared that numerous individuals and living beings would take my help, would stand with the power of my legs and follow the directions of my movements. The covering indicates that it would be for infinite and unknown period.

The fourth dream that I had was colourful. In that dream I saw four birds of different colours coming to me from different directions, falling at my feet and turning white.

It also indicated that people from all the four directions and all the four professions will come to me, take shelter and become one. There would be no difference and no discrimination. They would come for and will get *Nibbāna.*

The fifth dream was peculiar and strange too. I climbed a huge mountain of dung without being soiled by it.

Everything, whether solid or liquid, significant or insignificant, would help me ascend higher without mutilating me or dampening my image because I would always remain totally detached from them. None could soak me. They would form a base, pedestal for me to stand and ascend.

It is a fact that the dreams that are symbolic give greater satisfaction but it's also true that the dreams that are literally true give greater and instant pleasure. I remember one dream in which I saw an elephant serving me in many ways. Many decades later, one elephant called Pārileyaka actually served me during my three months long *ekāntavāsa*, when I lived alone. He brought for me water, flowers and fruits and kept company without disturbing me a lot. Later on, I mentioned it on many occasions that Pārileyaka has served me a lot; that such a companion in solitude is a boon and is pleasant. Even when such a companion is not there yet solitude is far better for a spiritual seeker. If the seeker gets a matured helper who accompanies during meditation, shows purity, displays patience and is alert and conscious after casting aside all the inner and outer fears, then he makes progress faster:

Sache labhetha nipakam sahāyam, saddhim charam sādhu vihāri dheeram;

Abhibhuyya sabbāni parissayāni, charya tenattamano sateemā.

But even if a seeker does not get such helpful companion he must move alone like a defeated king who abandons his kingdom or like an elephant that moves alone in the forest:

No che labhetha nipakam sahāyam, saddhi charam vihāri dheeram;

Rājā va rattham vijitam pahāya, yeko charo mātang-ranjjeva nāgo.

It is always better for the seeker to make all-out efforts alone and in solitude. Taking the help of a fool will ruin the effort. Like an elephant, the seeker should alone move away from sins and have the least attachment to worldliness:

Yekassa charitam seyyo, natthi bāle sahāyatā;

Yeko chare na cha pāpāni kayirā, appossukko mātanga-ranjjeva nāgo.

The seeker must use his own power and prowess and should never depend on anyone or anything, not even his dreams.

BUDDHA WAITS FOR A FARMER

One day, just when I was about to begin the sermon, I saw a farmer coming towards me. He seemed restless and was looking all around as if searching for something. He had lost something important, costly and big; maybe a cow, buffalo or an ox. I waited for him. It was not good to begin the sermon when a lone figure was approaching hurriedly.

The farmer came and prostrated before me to pay homage, and yet was looking around. He did not stay back. He arose and left the place. Obviously, he was worried because of his loss.

The monks and lay persons were waiting for me to begin the sermon but the farmer was in my mind. I could not shake him off. I waited for him. After about two hours, I saw him coming with an ox. He came up, tied his ox to a tree, came to me, prostrated before me again to pay homage, arose, but instead of leaving the gathering, he sat down to listen to me. He looked tired and yet was fresh; satisfied and happy. I realized that he must be hungry. I called a monk and asked him to serve food to the farmer. I began the sermon, only when the farmer had finished his food and was seated relaxed, ready for the sermon.

"O Monks! O Householders! This farmer was eager to listen to me. He came here some two hours ago but was worried about his ox. He needed that ox more than anything else. He is dependent on it. So, he immediately went in search of his ox. After two hours of a tiring search, he came here again tired but happy that he had regained his ox. He was still eager to listen to me but had I begun the sermon, it would have fallen on deaf ears without making any mark on the heart and mind as the farmer was tired and hungry. I deliberately and knowingly waited for the farmer to be ready for the sermon, both physically and mentally.

I know, and I tell you: hunger is the worst disease. Other diseases go away after correct and persistent treatment but hunger continues and returns again and again. Even when we take adequate food during the day and night, it returns the next day with the same intensity and similar need of food. We feel hunger and take food everyday, yet hunger never vanishes permanently. So, I say, hunger is the worst disease.

Work hard to feed the body and the family to be and keep others healthy. It can be done by wisely reducing the food-intake to the bare minimum and by taking a little less than required food every day. Your food must be *swachha*, clean and fresh; *suswādu*, tasteful; *supāchya*, digestible and *swāsthyavardhak*, healthy.

I told you all these things to draw your attention towards the balanced thinking and approach of the farmer towards his personal life and needs, and also towards Dhamma. Such balance can be easily maintained with a bit of correct thinking and willful implementation. It is practical wisdom!

Since you all have waited for quite a long time, I will give you something important and lasting. I will discuss six things unsurpassed.

1. The seeing unsurpassed;
2. The hearing unsurpassed;
3. The gain unsurpassed;
4. The training unsurpassed;
5. The service unsurpassed; and
6. The recollection unsurpassed.

What is the seeing unsurpassed? Many people like to see, desire to see or go to see many different things at different places. But seeing does not mean seeing the outer world, the beautiful, big and grand things like elephants, horses, jewels, something here or something there. No, that is not seeing. One comes to see me or my disciples out of faith and love, serenely assured of refuge in the three jewels for his/ her purification of being, for passing beyond sorrow and lamentation, for the destruction of suffering and pain, for following the noble path, and for the realization of nibbāna. Only then is that seeing unsrupassed.

What is the hearing unsurpassed? The hearing of the sound of drum or lute or other musical instruments, or listening to wrong ideas is no hearing at all but when one comes to hear the Dhamma from me or my disciple out of faith and love, serenely assured of refuge in the three jewels for his/ her purification of being, for passing beyond sorrow and lamentation, for the destruction of suffering and pain, for following the noble path, and for the realization of nibbāna. Only then is that hearing unsurpassed.

What is the gain unsurpassed? Someone gets wealth, another one a child and yet another one a wife or this here or that there, but this is no gain. One comes to see me or my disciple out of faith and love, serenely assured of refuge in the three jewels for his/her purification of being, for passing beyond sorrow and lamentation, for the destruction of suffering and pain, for following the noble path, and for the realization of nibbāna. Only then is this called gain unsurpassed.

What is the training unsurpassed? One acquires training in controlling a horse or an elephant, a chariot or gets exceptional skill in swordsmanship or archery in this or that, but this training is no training. One comes to see me or my disciple out of faith and love, serenely assured of refuge in the three jewels for his/her purification of being, for passing beyond sorrow and lamentation, for the destruction of suffering and pain, for following the noble path, and for the realization of nibbāna. Only then is that training unsurpassed.

What is the service unsurpassed? One serves a king or a minister, a householder a Vaishya or a Brāhmin or someone here or another one there, but this is no service at all. One comes to see me or my disciple out of faith and love, serenely assured of refuge in the three jewels for his/her purification of being, for passing beyond sorrow and lamentation, for the destruction of suffering and pain, for following the noble path, and for the realization of nibbāna. Only then is that service unsurpassed.

What is the recollection unsurpassed? One recollects the gain of a wife or a child or of wealth or love, common, worldly, ignoble or unbeneficial, but it is not recollection. One comes to see me or my disciple out of faith and love, serenely assured of refuge in the three jewels for his/ her purification of being, for passing beyond sorrow and lamentation, for the destruction of suffering and pain, for following the noble path, and for the realization of nibbāna. Only then is that recollection is unsurpassed.

Material gain and accumulation is neither a gain nor accumulation. If one does meritorious deeds after collecting wisdom and purifies oneself and then freedom from suffering and pain, one finally attains nibbāna. Then that gain and accumulation is meaningful and worthy.

Be conscious, meditate and think deeply to know what is right and what is wrong; what should be done and what are the things that are never to be taken; what are the deeds that purify and what are the things that make one fall into a lower order. Try to be better and better every day by performing only meritorious deeds.

Now, this is all for the day for your clear conception and better life, for healthier inner growth, to get rid of *ghrinā*, hatred; *lobha*, greed and *bhrama*, delusion, and for freedom from the *chakra*, (cycle) of incessant birth, suffering, lamentation, death and rebirth in the realms of insects, animals, ghosts or humans; and finally to attain nibbāna. *Sāmayikam pi vibhutim.*"

DHAMMA CHAKRA PARIVARTAN

I belong to the Shākya clan but I'm the Buddha, the one who is fully awake. This awakening did not come to me easily. Nothing great comes easily. Awakening is a rare phenomenon. It is enlightenment. It is becoming the light of knowledge: total light; complete knowledge; lacking nothing; getting overwhelmed. Even a minimum of contemplation over it fills one up to the brim with overwhelming cosmic power. It is indeed rare. Buddhas are rare. The Enlightened Ones are rare. A person becomes a Buddha but in myriads of millennia. Of course, my enlightenment happened in one day but I had put in many years of strenuous and unremitting effort. Not only in this life, but over countless previous lives I had been striving for revelation and awakening into the Universal and Absolute Truth. During the course of all those lives, I had been preparing myself for this enlightenment. I accumulated merit for three incalculable Manvantar, aeons of time. A Manvantar is a great method of calculating time span of billions of years that rise and fall in extremely long Yugas, cycles within infinity of Time. With that accumulated merit I could achieve it in this life after many years of rigorous learning, practice and meditation and 39 days of *Hatha Sādhanā* under a tree in Uruvelā near Gayā. I was ready for awakening but not for self mortification. Self mortification defeats the purpose. I had renounced everything for it, for searching the path to wipe out suffering from life. So I concentrated on what I was looking for. I attained such a concentration that in earth I was not percipient of earth; in water I was not percipient of water; in fire I was not percipient of fire; in air I was not percipient of air. It became the base of the infinity of space. It became the base of the infinity of consciousness. It became the very basis of nothingness; the base of neither perception, nor non-perception. I was not in the world and yet I was in the world; I was not in the world beyond and yet I was in the world and everything simultaneously. Yet I perceived. It was the perception of non-perception; even non-perception was perceived.

Even during that hour of intense concentration, I was conscious of the fact that awakening has no parallel. It is the rarest among all achievements. I will have to sustain under all sorts of duress. The greater the goal, the greater the effort needed to accomplish that. I knew difficulties would come; fear, doubt and darkness would try its level best to displace me. I did not allow digression. I had been fighting against Māra, had defeated him time and again and yet Māra was not leaving me. I had to be on the right track to defeat Māra forever. I was sure of the victory ahead. That inner confidence kept me on the track of search for the path. I did it. I got it. I have it. Māra failed to create strong delusion and wrong belief around me. The defeated Māra returned with his train. He accepted his defeat. Then, the darkness around me started thinning, then thinning faster, then almost vanishing until it finally vanished. There was no trace of darkness in that deep forest among the big banyan trees, smaller plants and numerous creepers moving ahead or rising high along the trees and branches or falling down from there. They were quite clearly visible. I was able to see and feel them on my mental plane even when I had closed my eyes. I was able to see distant things very closely, in detail and in crystal clear form. I felt them entering inside me and settling.

Enlightenment

I was left in solitude but I was not alone. I was with trees, leaves, fruits, grass and the living beings around. I was one with Nature, one with Cosmos, one with the earth and with the sky. Then

I started getting light; light from all around. It was all light. I was light. I became light. I am light. There was light. There is light in me as much as there is light outside me. I am still a part of the cosmic light. I was not alone, I was with light and in light; a lighted being; an enlightened one.

There was light, light and only light: light of knowledge; light of life; life of the cosmos; the light connecting the inner light with the cosmic light. It was the beginning of revelation and it lasted till the completion of awakening and even after that. The light is still in me, around me.

Then it dawned on me. It came as light. Everything dawned on me. Then I perceived all. Everything was revealed to me. I got everything. I got all knowledge. I got all wisdom. It was immense and infinite and continues to be so. It is Truth: Universal and Absolute.

The realization of the ultimate truth of reality unfolded in stages like a illuminated lotus unfurling its petals. It was the lotus of light. I had already crossed many stages of detached and calm thinking, and was somewhere in the supra-conscious state. The chatter of mind was over a long time back. I was somewhere in the transcended thought, ready to enter the state of exalted rapture; of the purest joy and purest and complete knowledge. It continued to evade me but then opened up like a myriad of illuminated petals of innumerable lotuses of light. There was peaceful upheaval; tempestuous tranquility; soundless speed of light and the illuminated silence of Cosmos. All of them opened up with supernatural fastness and flawless culmination. from the tinniest to the biggest; from me to all; from the tree to infinity. All and each came to me. I'm all and each. Infinity was now in me. I was infinity. I am infinity with the wisdom. Wisdom will stay with me. Wisdom will live in me with infinity.

Experiences tell us that our conflict, distress and suffering emanate from the lack of knowledge and wisdom. For changing information and knowledge into wisdom, one must examine them in the light of different traditions that human beings follow in different regions and context. Intelligence, cleverness and dynamism are the qualities a person can be born with but wisdom is to be acquired by deep meditation over the existing and collected knowledge. This is the best way to move from raw information to refined thinking, cultured feeling, sublime reflections and compassionate deeds. Refined thinking produces awareness, the discerning power and keeps interest alive. It helps in sustaining during duress. If one is responsive to the feelings and information one can process them in positive ways, but if one reacts, then introspection, intuition and analysis will lose both the depth and loftiness. The wisdom is best expressed in committed, passionate, wise, wholesome, fair and effective actions. Discernment is the power to discern between wrong and right; just and unjust; constructive and destructive and wholesome and unwholesome. Discernment is the essence of wisdom. The wisdom that dawned upon me enriched me. I am complete and perfect.

Finding the Path

From that infinity I found the path; a clear path of Eight Noble Truths. From that infinity I found four Noble Truths. Only after knowing that Truth and by following that path, which I have discovered anyone can be free from suffering. It is the path between normal and abnormal life. It is the Middle Path, the *Majjhim Māgga.*

Now, I have to share this insight with others. I acquired it so that I may share it with others. If it is not shared then there is no use of and meaning in *Buddhattva* or enlightenment. My enlightenment is for others. I had forsaken my palace for others. I have to go to others and give it to them; to them all or to as many as possible before my final departure, my Parinirvān, my Mahāparinirvān. The path is definite and a journey on it is to be seen, done and felt by one and all. I have to show the path and make others move on that path: the path to Nibbāna.

I must share my knowledge with others. It is for others. Although, after enlightenment, nothing remains to be attained; but for the sake of sharing I must visit others and teach them. It is not for my personal use and gain. It is for the benefit of others, for their use so that they can be free from fear and suffering; from impurities and the cycle of birth and rebirth. Enlightenment is not a personal gain. The power so gained and the energy thus absorbed becomes the power and energy of the human race. That is how man has grown to this lofty height of wisdom and accomplishment. The wisdom gained and the knowledge accumulated by one person remains neither his personal creation nor private collection. Thousands of men have striven hard for thousands of years, and have added drop by drop to existing drops. By sharing knowledge, the mental faculty of human beings will be enriched. It is a subtle and indirect process in a direct way. This will improve the life of millions of people in every millennium. They will learn many things including the much needed contentment, and will be able to distinguish between the worthless, crude and demanding and human, spiritual and sublime.

Despite the fact that my five disciples deserted me there and returned to lead a life of their own liking I did not abandon what I was doing. I knew a path would emerge from that path. I was in search of the path. I got the path. It is between self mortification and the material riches. One has to do away with the extremes. Extremes are something that cause fall. I had to avoid the extreme. I did it and accepted the *Ksheer Bhojanam* from Sujātā. That milky preparation was pure. It was a purifier too. I had those five dreams. I knew the meaning of the dreams. I was sure. I have been sure.

With the enlightenment, I have become a normal man but I have unlocked my potential, the inner cosmic energy and have directly perceived the Truth, the true nature of things. This unlocking of inner cosmic power and its tremendous and continuous flow makes everything appear abnormal. Normal insight is different and only a bit deeper than the superficial insight but enlightenment reveals the Truth. What a strange thing! The abnormal act of striving for revelation made me normal. In that normalcy, I saw and realized the middle path, the balanced one. Yes, achieving balance in life is a state of happiness and bliss.

I had been sitting in one posture, my favourite lotus posture, and meditating on various aspects of life for 39 days in a row; when one day, the full moon day of Vaishākha that the enlightenment dawned upon me. It comes to my mind again and again. Every time I get a similar light, not of that magnitude, yet immense. I am filled up with light, the light of knowledge and wisdom. I could see nothing else. There was and there is light and light everywhere. The days were full of light and the nights too were full of light. There was virtually no dark place in the forest. Even the shadows of the trees were lighted. I absorbed that light. I had to absorb that light. The light had to be in me and for me to enable me to share that light of wisdom with others. How could I absorb all that light and how could I share that light with others, was the biggest question before me after enlightenment. I wanted to obtain the answer and obtain it before I left that place. The answer was stuck in the form of glowing light around my head in the form of a halo. It was the halo that indicated my enlightenment.

Staying Back

I remained at Uruvelā for four weeks after enlightenment thinking over the events and digesting the whole range of fresh and new wisdom.

The trees were the first to know and feel my enlightenment. Trees and plants are more sensitive than living beings. They are sensitive to moisture, air and heat too.

Then the birds came to know of the enlightenment and gave their acceptance and declared their knowledge and feeling by chirping for hours every day around me.

The next to know about it were the animals. They have their perception through smell. It takes time, for air is the only means by which they obtain their smell. Many animals came, made soothing sounds and sat around for hours then dispersed to come again the next day.

Then people nearby got the inkling. They started coming in small and large groups. They expected me to say something but I said nothing.

I sat for one week under one banyan tree and another week at yet another. That way, I sat under four different peepal trees in four weeks. At each place I arranged different ideas in different ways. They were different sets. I was not able to speak. The cause behind my silence was not physical weakness but overwhelming knowledge, wisdom and experience. New and different ideas were flowing fast in me. I had to control their flow and arrange the ideas in a coherent whole. It took time.

The First Discourse

Then I went in search of my teachers, preceptors and disciples. I went to the residence of Alara Kalama. I was informed that the learned guru had died a week ago. Then I went to my other guru Uddaka Rāmaputra. When I reached there I got the sad news that he had departed for the other world the last evening.

Then I remembered my disciples. I had five disciples: Kaundinna; Appa; Bhaddiya; Mahānām and Ashwajeet. They are very young and energetic. They are wise and very confident orators. They are ascetics. They returned to the town when they found me deep in meditation for many days to find panacea for the evils of suffering. I acquired my original five disciples. They met me at Isipatanā which is also known as Rishipatan in a deer garden, Mriga Dāo called Mriga Vātikā. It is a nice garden at the centre. They addressed me by name and called *āruso*, friend, a common address. I immediately corrected them:

"O Ascetics! Don't address the Tathāgata by name or by friendly 'aruso'. I'm the Tathāgata, the Exalted One. I'm now the Enlightened One. Lend your ears. O Ascetics! Deathlessness has been attained! Now, I shall teach the Dhamma and activate the Dhamma Chakka, the Wheel of Religion with the teaching of Dhamma. If you act according to my instructions, before long you will realize by your own intuitive knowledge and wisdom, and attain in this life itself, the Supreme Consummation of the holy life."

My original disciples were wise. They were not stubborn. They became aware of the light around me of the heat, energy and wisdom that I emitted by Truth and Boodha-hood. They agreed to listen to me and follow my instructions.

Precisely two months after my Enlightenment I could utter something. I was ready and delivered the first discourse to the group of those original disciples, the five ascetics who had abandoned me earlier.

With this discourse, I set that Wheel of Dhamma that I had got, moving. I activated the Wheel of Dhamma: *Dhamma chakka Pavattana*. I expounded the Dhamma in the Mriga Vātikā, the Deer Park in Isipatnāranya; Isipatana, Rishipatan near Vārānasi, *Aghanāshi, Avināshi* Kāshi, the place that cleanses sins, purifies, glorifies and makes immortal.

The intellectual five monks, the ascetics and my original disciples, who were closely associated with me for six years till I settled in the Uruvelā forest before the enlightenment, were the only human beings that were present to hear my first sermon. Many other invisible beings such as Devas and Brahmas were also present on that great occasion, but were invisible to others. First I felt their presence and then I saw them. The wisdom of enlightenment is rare, even for the celestial spirits. So they took advantage of the golden opportunity of listening to the first sermon. But I directly addressed my sermon to the five ascetics and the discourse was intended mainly for them; and to the human world through them.

The halo around my head had attracted the animals and birds. Instinctively they knew something rare was to happen in the Mriga Vātikā. So the birds and animals had come in large numbers. I could clearly perceive that all the deer of the park were sitting silently around us. The trees were full of birds. Some birds were also playing around the deer. Some of them were jumping and chirping but I felt a lot of cadence in their movements and sound. It was never cacophonous. I had seen earlier in another garden only a fistful of birds making a lot of noise. But I felt that there was no noise in the deer park. There was no sadness too. There was pleasure and happiness all around the park. The birds and animals had come either to see me or listen to me, or both. They may not understand human language but they have their own way of knowing things and can even distinguish between the friendly and the inimical.

Definitely, they had some legitimate share in my knowledge and wisdom. It was not limited only to human beings, but was and is for all living beings. All living beings have their decent share in the Dhamma that I am to expound, activate, propound and teach to the world. I will activate and make the Wheel of Dhamma, move for all. It is the founding of and the establishment of wisdom. Dhamma is the Truth and the Truth is the Dhamma. It is the turning of the Wheel of Truth; activating the Wheel of Dhamma; or Setting the Wheel of Dhamma in motion.

In this most important discourse, in the very beginning I cautioned my disciples to avoid two extremes. I said: "There two extremes which should not be resorted to by a recluse who has renounced the world. One extreme is constant attachment to sensual pleasures. This extreme is base, vulgar, worldly and ignoble. It is profit-less. This extreme of self-indulgence retards spiritual progress of the recluse and ascetic.

Another extreme that one must avoid is self-mortification, which weakens the intellect. This extreme is not practised by the ordinary man. It is painful, ignoble, and profitless. Unlike the first extreme this is not base, worldly, or vulgar. I say this based on my experience of this profitless course. It is useless. It only multiplies suffering instead of diminishing it.

By realizing the mistake of both these two extremes, a middle path can be taken and followed. I have discovered this new path by myself. This new system is "*Majjhima patipāda*", the Middle Path.

The two diametrically opposite extremes must be rejected. This middle path must be followed because it produces spiritual insight and intellectual wisdom. It enables to see things as they truly are. When insight is clarified and the intellect is sharpened, everything is seen in its true perspective. Furthermore, the Middle Path leads to the subjugation of passions and the multiplying of wisdom and peace. Above all, it leads to the attainment of the four supra-mundane paths; Knowledge of Sainthood, to the understanding of the Four Noble Truths and finally to the realization of the Ultimate Goal, Nibbāna.

Noble Eightfold Path

Dear Disciples! Now, what is the Middle Path? It is the Noble Eightfold Path. There are eight factors of this Noble Path. They are:

The first factor is Right Understanding. This is the keynote of Dhamma. Right Understanding will clear the doubts and pave the track on the right way and right direction.

Right Understanding deals with knowledge of oneself as one really is; as well as that of the world and other human and non-human beings in the right perspective without excessively rejecting anything or anyone or without showing excessive attachment to anyone or anything. Those are the two extreme poles that one must avoid to lead a balanced life in the middle, by adopting and following the middle path.

The second factor is the Right Thinking. In absence of the right thinking there cannot be clear vision and right work. Clear vision leads to clear thinking; and clear thinking leads to clear and rightful living and doing. Hence right thinking becomes an important factor of the Noble Eightfold Path. This mental state may be called "initial application", which affects all the deeds. This important mental state eliminates wrong ideas or emotions and helps the other moral adjuncts to be directed towards Nibbāna.

Samma Sankappa, Right Thought and determination; serves the dual purpose of eliminating evil thoughts and developing pure thoughts. But its best application lies in the fact that it controls the deeds, directs the mind and energy towards correct and beneficial deeds and distracts mind from wrong and negative deeds. In this particular connection, Right Thought is three-fold:

a. *Nekkhamma Sankappa*: The Thought of Renunciation of worldly pleasures or the thought of selflessness. This is opposed to attachment, selfishness, and self-possessiveness. That way, it creates sympathy and compassion.

b. *Abhayapada Sankappa*: The thought of loving kindness or benevolence which is opposed to hatred, ill-will, or aversion. This creates the idea of sameness and brotherhood among human beings and the feelings to save the non-human beings.

c. *Abhihimsā Sankappa*: The thought of harmlessness or compassion, which is opposed to cruelty and callousness. The sense and determination of non-violence soothes the nerves and makes living among the other living beings possible and easy. Tensions are erased and the realization is strengthened in us that they are also like us: living, growing, and waging their struggle for existence.

Many evil and good forces are latent in all mankind. As long as we are interested in and attached to worldly things, these evil forces rise to the surface at unexpected moments in disconcerting strength. When once they are totally eradicated even before attaining full enlightenment, one's stream of consciousness becomes perfectly purified.

He whose mind is free from selfish desires, hatred and cruelty, and is saturated with spirit of selflessness, loving kindness, and harmlessness, lives in perfect peace. He is indeed a blessing to himself and others. Such a person is of the right thinking.

The third factor is Right Speech: Right Thought leads to Right Speech. Right speech means refraining from false speech, slandering, harsh words and frivolous talk. That which is true and pleasant is the right speech: *satyam vada priyam vada*. If the thinking is negative or prejudiced then one cannot tell the truth. Wrong thinking leads to falsehood and thus to pain and suffering.

People should be truthful and trustworthy and should ever seek the good and beautiful in others, instead of deceiving, defaming, denouncing or disuniting them. A harmless mind generated by loving kindness cannot give vent to harsh speech, which first defaces the speaker and then hurts others. Whatever one utters must be true, and also sweet and pleasant, useful, fruitful, beneficial and acceptable to others.

The fourth factor is Right Action. Right Action follows Right Speech. If the speech is not right then the action cannot be soothing, helpful and beneficial to all. Right Action entails refraining from killing, stealing, immoral conduct and sexual misconduct. All such evil deeds are caused by craving and anger, lust and jealousy. These are associated with ignorance too. By gradually eliminating these causes from the mind one can get rid of blameworthy actions. Such misconducts will not find expression. A person who is determined to do only right action will remain aloof from all sorts of lust, jealousy, anger, revenge and unethical deeds. Being pure in mind, a person will lead a pure life. Purity of one thing leads to the purity of another and so on, till one's entire life is purged. It takes place with right action.

The fifth factor is Right Livelihood. If everything else is good, pure and ethical but one's very livelihood is based on immoral earning, misconduct and crime or any other thing against human or non-human beings, then that life will be full of misery. That is not a good life and a person earning livelihood by wrong means is not a good person and can never attain *nibbāna.* If purifying view, thoughts, words, and deeds absorbed at the outset then the spiritual pilgrim can try to purify his livelihood. For purifying one's livelihood one must refrain from five kinds of trade. What are they? I declare that one must refrain from getting engaged in these five kinds of trade. These are: Trading in weapons; trading in human beings, trading after slaughtering animals and trading in intoxicants, intoxicating drinks and drugs. To show an appreciation for the beauty of life, all should abstain from these five kinds of improper trade.

The sixth factor is Right Effort. Success depends on right effort. One may be working hard but may lack skill and knowledge and hence unable to make the right effort, then he or she is not able to accomplish anything. His works will not be completed. After making a lot of wrong effort he will leave the work unfinished. But if right effort is made with right earnestness the task will be completed in due course. In this sense, right effort is fourfold, namely:

a. The endeavour to prevent the arising of evils not yet arisen.

b. The endeavour to discard evil that has already arisen.

c. The endeavour to cultivate good not yet arisen.

d. The endeavour to develop the good that has already arisen.

Right Effort plays a very important part in the Noble Eightfold Path. It is by one's own effort that deliverance is obtained; not by seeking refuge in others or by offering prayers.

Men possess both virtues and evils. Both a rubbish-heap of evil and a storehouse of virtue are found in men. By Right Effort one removes the rubbish-heap and cultivates the seeds of latent virtues. The seeds of virtues sprout and take the shape and form of a tree – green, leafy and growing. These virtues make him good and keep him so. That way he begets health and happiness and respect from friends, relatives, neighbours and foes.

The seventh factor is Right Mindfulness. Right Effort is closely associated with Right Mindfulness. Mindfulness is correct thought, judgment, opinion, purpose, inclination, direction and attention. It is that which thinks attentively; knows the truth and reality; feels the need and happenings and wills to perform. It is an inner composition that affects one's thinking and effort. It is mindfully doing things. It is constant mindfulness with regard to body, feelings, thoughts and mind objects that shapes the ideas and makes the effort possible. Mindfulness of these four objects tends to eradicate misconceptions with regard to desirability, so-called happiness, permanence and an immortal soul.

The eighth factor is Right Concentration. Right concentration helps the mind to come to a common centre; to focus, to direct the attention on to the matter in hand; to direct thoughts and efforts towards one object and to remain fixed on something. Right Effort and Right Mindfulness lead to Right Concentration, which is one-pointed-ness of mind. A concentrated mind acts as a powerful aid to see things as they truly are by means of penetrative insight and decides to make right effort as it rightly understands the given thing, idea or situation.

I also explained to them that of these eight factors of the Noble Eightfold Path, the first two are for **wisdom**, the second three are for the growth of **morality** in the inner being, and the last three are for **concentration**. According to the order of development, Sīla, Morality, Samādhi, Concentration, and Panna, Wisdom are the three stages on the Noble Path. All these factors denote the mental attitude of the aspirant who will strive to gain Deliverance.

Four Noble Truths

Having prefaced the discourse with a description of the two extremes and my newly discovered Middle Path, I expounded the **Four Noble Truths** in detail.

I gave them four great and perennial Truths, *Sanātana Satya.* Sachcha, or Satya or Truth means 'what really is'. These are the foundations of my teaching, which are associated with the life of all beings, particularly the life of all human beings. Hence, this doctrine is homo-centric, in contrast to theo-centric. My teaching is inward looking rather than outward looking. These Truths always exist whether anyone realizes it or not. I, the Buddha, perceive them and reveal these to the deluded world. Nobody can change them: no time, no space, or no person can change or replace them because they are Ultimate Truths. I did not depend upon anyone for my realization of the Noble Truths. They came to me; rather, dawned on me.

In that first discourse I explained and established the originality of my teachings. I said, "With regard to this Dhamma unheard before, there arose in me the eye; the knowledge, the wisdom, the insight and the light". These are *Ārsha Satya*, the Noble Truths, original and perennial truth.

I said, "**The First Noble Truth** is dukkha, pain which means suffering or misery. Here, "du" means emptiness and "kha" means feeling. Dukkha therefore, means the feeling of emptiness. Average men see the outer form of the things and remain limited to the surface. They are only surface-seers. An Arya sees things as they truly are. To an Arya, all life is suffering and he finds no real happiness in this world, which otherwise deceives mankind with illusory pleasures. Material happiness is merely the gratification of some desire. It is limited to physical pleasure and physical aspect of life.

All beings are subject to *jāti*, birth; *jara*, decay; *vyādhi*, disease; and finally to *mrityu*, death. No one is exempt from these four causes of suffering. Birth is suffering, decay is suffering, disease is suffering and death is suffering. Unfulfilled wishes are also suffering. As a rule, everybody wishes to be associated either with beloved ones or pleasant things. This is attachment. Attachment causes suffering. Nobody wishes to be associated with hated ones or unpleasant things. We always wish to be associated with persons or things we like. However, our cherished desires are not always gratified. At times what we least expect or least desire is thrust on us. Sometimes, such unexpected unpleasant circumstances become so intolerable and painful that weak and ignorant people are compelled to commit suicide; as if such an act would solve the problems of life. It is no way to live and fight suffering. It is also no way to get rid of suffering. One can get rid of suffering only by following the noble Eightfold Path.

Real happiness is found within and it is not defined in terms of wealth, power, honours or conquests. If such worldly possessions are forcibly or unjustly obtained or are misdirected or even viewed with attachment, they become a source of misery and sorrow for the possessors.

Normally, the enjoyment of sensual pleasures is the highest and only happiness for average human beings. There is some momentary happiness in the anticipation, gratification, and retrospection of such fleeting material pleasure, but this is illusory and temporary. Non-attachment, *virāga* to material pleasure, or transcending material pleasure is bliss. This composite body of clinging is itself a great heap of manifold suffering.

The Second Noble Truth is *Samudaya*, the origin of suffering; the cause and origin of the first noble truth. Right Understanding can be explained as the knowledge of the four Noble Truths too. These Truths are concerned with this one-fathom long body of man. Right understanding of the first Noble Truth leads to the eradication of the second Noble Truth which is the origin of the first Noble Truth.

One who searches for supra-mundane happiness and final liberation must understand that the first Noble Truth is to be penetrated, the Second Noble Truth to be eradicated, the Third Noble Truth is to be realized and the Fourth Noble Truth is to be followed. This is Right Understanding, the keynote of Dhamma.

It is this craving that produces rebirth, accompanied by passionate clinging, delight now here in this life, then there in that life. It is the craving for sensual pleasures, craving for existence, and craving for non-existence.

There are three kinds of craving. The first is the grossest form of craving, which is simple attachment to all sensual pleasures, *kāmatanhā*. The second is attachment to existence, *bhāvatanhā*. It is the pleasure that one derives from ideas, thinking of other things and remembering them. Hence, it is an attachment to the realms of form, *rupa tanhā*; and also as attachment to formless realms, *arupatanhā*. The third is attachment to non-existence, *vibhāva tanhā*. Of the three, the second craving is attachment to sensual pleasures connected with the belief in eternal setting, *sāssataditthi*, and the third craving is attachment to sensual pleasures connected with the belief in nihilism, *echchhedāditthi*.

Craving is a powerful mental force latent in all beings. It is the chief cause of most of the miseries of life. This craving, gross or subtle, leads to repeated births in a cycle of continuity of suffering. This craving makes beings cling to all forms of life. Right Understanding of the First Noble Truth leads to the eradication of craving, and so releases one from suffering.

The Third Noble Truth is *nirodha,* the cessation of suffering. This, the Noble Truth of the cessation of suffering, is the complete separation from, and destruction of this very craving; its forsaking, renunciation, libration from everything, and it results in non-attachment, or is gained through non-attachment. This Third Noble Truth is a complete cessation of suffering, which is Nibbāna, the ultimate goal of Dhamma. Nibbāna can be achieved in this very life by the total eradication of all forms of craving. This Nibbāna is to be realized by renouncing all attachment to the internal body and external world.

This First Truth of suffering which depends on this so-called being and various aspects of life is to be carefully examined, analyzed, and understood. This examination leads to a proper understanding of oneself as one really is. The cause of this suffering is craving or attachment. From craving springs grief; from craving springs fear; for the individual who is wholly free from craving, there is no grief, much less fear.

This Third Truth of the cessation of suffering is to be realized by developing the Noble Eightfold Path.

The Fourth Noble Truth is mārga, the way leading to the cessation from suffering. When a person develops properly the Noble Eightfold Path, he can eradicate craving, which is the cause of suffering. When he eradicates craving, he can completely stop the continuous cycle of suffering. When this craving and this suffering are removed completely, one can realize Nibbāna. This is the power of the Noble Eightfold Path. This unique path is the only straight way to Nibbāna.

Expounding the four Noble Truths in various ways I concluded the discourse with these forcible words: "Ascetics! Till the absolute true intuitive knowledge, regarding these four Noble Truths under their three aspects, and twelve modes, was not perfectly clear to me, I did not accept or announce that I had gained incomparable Supreme Enlightenment."

Dhamma Chakka Pavattana

"When the absolute true intuitive knowledge regarding these Four Noble Truths became perfectly clear to me, only then I decided to declare that I had gained incomparable Supreme Enlightenment; only then I came to you to teach Dhamma and activate a new Dhamma Chakka."

"There arose in me the knowledge and insight; unshakable is the deliverance of my mind, this is my last birth, and now there is no existence again."

"When I expounded the discourse of the *Dhammachakka*, the earth-bound deities exclaimed, I heard them clearly: "This excellent *Dhammachakka*, which could not be expounded by any ascetic, priest, god, Māra or Brahma in this world, has been expounded by the Enlightened and Exalted One at this Deer Park, Mriga Vātikā, at Isipatana in Vārānasi, the celestial abode."

"Hearing this, Devas and Brahmas of all the other planes also shouted the same in joyous chorus. A radiant light, surpassing the light of gods, appeared in the world. It was the light of the Dhamma. It illumined the whole world, and brought instant peace and inner happiness to all beings. All were relieved and felt at ease."

There was an immediate and lasting effect of this teaching. There was change all around. The five ascetics also felt sublimity. Kaundinya, the senior of the five disciples, understood the Dhamma and attained *sovan,* the first stage of Sainthood whereby he realized that whatever is subject to origination is also the subject to cessation: *Yam kinchid samudaya dhammam sarvam tam nirodha dhammam.* Later on, when the other four ascetics started following the instructions, they too attained the same state. It was the first stage of their spiritual eminence. It had a lasting effect. This effect gave its final result when they heard the *Attālakkhana Sutta*, which deals with *anatthā*, soullessness, all those five Brāhmin ascetics attained *Arhantship*, the final stage of sainthood before *Nibbāna.*

No one, neither the humans nor non-humans; neither the Devas nor the other supernatural beings left that place for quite a long time, though the discourse was over. They were engrossed in Dhamma; in the Dhamma Chakka that had started moving.

INITIATION

It was a nice day. I had moved from village to village and had talked to many common and distinguished persons. I had given many short speeches at different places. When I move from place to place, I prefer to be brief so that I can move ahead. Yet the eager listeners want something. They expect me to give them the essence. They have their duties. They are somehow busy in something. They were not ready for a longer discourse. I know it. I have experienced it. I know life. Their lives are not an exception.

Change is Perennial

At one place, some people were talking about changes in life and mind of a person. It was brought to my knowledge. They wanted to know: 'why has that man changed so much?' They don't realize that change is the only unchangeable system of Nature. Hence, everything is temporal. There is nothing permanent in the world, the Universe, the different *lokas*, and galaxies.

I told them that eight worldly conditions keep the world turning around. The strange thing is that the world keeps on turning around these eight worldly conditions.

They had asked: What are those worldly conditions?'

I replied: "Those are the four pairs of condition, definitely opposite in the pair. They are:

gain and loss;

fame and disrepute;

praise and blame

pleasure and pain.

These eight worldly conditions are encountered by both the uninstructed laymen and by instructed noble disciples. One can ask 'what are the distinction, difference, disparity or dividing factors between an uninstructed layman and a noble instructed disciple?

The difference and distinction are very clear. When an uninstructed layman acquires gain he does not reflect on it in an intelligent fashion. He does not think that the gain that has come to him is impermanent, subject to change and bound with suffering. In the same way, when an uninstructed layman faces loss; blame and notoriety or is famous or praised, he does not think in a wise and intelligent way thus that whatever has come to him is impermanent, subject to change and bound with suffering. He does not know the reality. He does not know them as they really are. All these worldly conditions keep his mind so much engrossed that he is unable to think in a clear and balanced way. It is because he is an uninstructed layman. He is elated with praise and fame and aggrieved at the loss and blame. He is either elated or dejected. Because he is still engrossed in likes and dislikes, he will not get freedom from birth. He will remain deeply affected by ageing and death; sorrow, lamentation, pain, grief, despair, luxury, pleasure, wealth and hence will continue to die and take birth.

But when an instructed noble disciple acquires gain, he reflects upon it in a positive manner like this: The gain that has come to me is impermanent. It will change, it will perish, it will not stay with me. It is subject to change and it is bound with suffering. He knows the reality. He knows what these things really are. These worldly conditions will not keep his mind engrossed so he is able to think in a clear and balanced way. He will reflect in the same vein when he faces loss; blame, notoriety or is famous or praised. He thinks in wise and intelligent ways that whatever has come to him is subject to change; is impermanent and bound with suffering. He is not engrossed in likes and dislikes. So, he is closer to Arhantship; to attain total freedom from birth and death. He can achieve it in this very life or he may have to come to this world for one or two times but he will always remain unaffected by ageing and death; sorrow and lamentation, pain and grief, luxury and pleasure, and wealth and accumulation of wealth.

People don't think of the impermanence of the things. They consider all the gains to be permanent and the loss as permanent too. Therefore, they feel elated at gain and morose at loss. On the other hand, instructed noble disciples think of those things. This is the distinction, difference, disparity and distinguishing features between them."

Aims and Objects

I had come back to the place where I was staying at that time. It was a moonlit night. A Brāhmin Jānushoni was waiting for me. He approached me, paid homage and said: "O Honourable Shākya Muni Gautam! I have some doubts. Please clarify them"

It has always been a pleasure when some persons come with some questions. At least, it is clear that they have been thinking on my teachings. They are satisfied on many counts yet they have their curiosity. They have some new questions. Their queries must be answered. I said: "O Brāhmin! Be comfortable! Sit at ease! Be relaxed. Then you can ask your questions one by one. I will answer them all."

When he was seated and others had also taken their respective places, Brāhmin Jānushoni asked: "What is a noble man's aim? What is his quest, his mainstay, his desire and his ideas?"

I looked at the gathering then turned towards the Brāhmin and patiently gave him the answer: "O Brāhmin! Wealth is a noble man's aim. His quest is for knowledge. His mainstay is power and his desire is to rule the earth. His ideal is sovereignty."

"O Arhant! It is great. I get it. Please tell me, what is a Brāhmin's aim? What is his quest and mainstay? What is his desire and what is his ideal?"

I gave him the reply to his second query without changing the tone and without taking my eyes off his face: "wealth is a Brāhmin's aim. His quest is for knowledge and wisdom. His mainstay is the sacred texts. His desire is for sacrifices and his ideal is the Brahma-world."

"It is great! O! Enlightened One! I get it. Now I want to know, what is a householder's aim? What is his quest, mainstay, ideal and desire?"

In the same tone and tempo, I gave the reply: "Wealth is a householder's aim. His quest is for knowledge. His mainstay is his craft. His desire is for work and his ideal idea is to finish the work at hand."

"O Great! Shākya Muni! Please tell me what is the aim of a woman? What is her quest and mainstay? What is her desire and ideal in life?

I said, "A man is a woman's aim. Her quest is for luxury and adornment. Her mainstay is her son who secures her life in the society. Her desire is to be with a husband without a co-wife. Her ideal is domination."

"Now tell me O great and wise ascetic," said the Brāhmin, "What is the aim of a thief? What is his quest and mainstay? What is his desire and ideal?"

"O Brahmin!" I replied, "Robbery is the aim of a thief. His quest is for a hiding place where he can keep the theft safe and when needed where he can himself hide. Weapons are his mainstay. He desires for darkness and his ideal is not to be ever caught."

"O Great Master! I have a last question, please answer it. What is an ascetic's aim? What is his quest and mainstay? What is his desire and ideal?"

The Brāhmin was really satisfied with all the answers and so declared in the presence of all. I kept on looking at him and gave the answer: "O Brāhmin! Hear carefully! Patience and purity is an ascetic's aim. His quest is for knowledge and wisdom. Virtue is his mainstay. His desire is not to be hampered, embarrassed or encumbered. His ideal is definitely Nibbāna, freedom from the cycle of birth-death and rebirth."

The Brāhmin said: "O Enlightened One! It is great! You have answered all my queries well. You have given the right and correct answers regarding the aim, quest, mainstay, desire and ideal of Brāhmins, householders, women, thieves and ascetics. O Arhant! Your replies have satisfied me."

Saying so, Brāhmin Jānushoni fell at my feet, prostrated and requested: "O Great One! Please accept me as a lay follower! Let me take refuge in the Dhamma until my life's end. I must know and serve Dhamma for the rest of my life."

Pabbajjā: Initiation

I placed my right palm over his head, "O Brāhmin! I accept you as a lay devotee! The initiation will take place here and now!"

This was enough of indication for the monks who patiently and meticulously well made all the arrangements of the initiation of Brāhmin Jānushoni.

The monks knew and followed the process of admission to the **sangha** involves two distinct acts: ***pabbajjā***, lower ordination, which consists of renunciation of secular life and acceptance of monastic life as a novice, and **upasampada,** higher ordination, official consecration as a monk. There is no need to clarify anything. These two acts are performed and occur at the same time. The Brāhmin was welcome "*Ehi bhikkhu*," "Come, O Monk!"

To accept him into the fold his head was shaved as was his beard. He was given the yellow robes of the monk. He bowed to the abbot who was a senior monk, to whom he made his oral petition for admittance. Then he sat with legs crossed and hands folded, pronouncing three times the formula of the Triple Refuge

"I take refuge in the *Buddha*!

I take refuge in the *Dhamma*!

I take refuge in the *Sangha!*"

He repeated after the officiating monk the Ten Precepts and vowed to observe them. In the presence of at least ten monks the Brāhmin was questioned in detail by the abbot: as to the name of teachers under whom he studied, whether he was free of faults and defects that would prevent his admission, and whether he had committed any henious sins, was diseased, mutilated, or was in debt. The abbot, when satisfied, thrice proposed acceptance of the oral petition. The Brāhmin's silence was treated as his consent. That way, Brāhmin Jānushoni was made a Bhikkhu.

ALERTNESS ALL THE TIME

Pure and Open Life

My life is open to all and known to all. There is nothing in it that is to be kept secret from others. It is a life for all. All must know it and must live with that openness. Like me, none should have anything to conceal.

I attained enlightenment because my bodily conduct is purified. With my body I have done nothing wrong, unethical or immoral. I have kept wrong-doing away from my life. In my whole life, I have nothing to conceal. With determination, anyone can achieve that merit in life.

My verbal conduct is thoroughly pure. Even in the palace I used no rough language for any one. Throughout my life, I have not used harsh words for anyone. One with such sweetness and purity in speech lives in absolute tranquility. It is not difficult for anyone to achieve this.

My mental conduct is pure. I have not allowed any wrong thought against other people to creep into my mind. In this regard, I have fought hard against Māra, who used all his weapons to plant something immoral or unethical in my mind, even with the help of his daughters but I was determined to defeat him. I accepted nothing and Māra was defeated. That is why my mental faculty is clean and mental conduct is pure. I have nothing to conceal.

I know, and even others know that there is nothing wrong with my livelihood. I have lived on whatever I got: the best of the food on one hand and leaves and fodder on the other. I have accepted those things without complaining. There too, I have nothing to conceal. My life is so open and so well known to others that I have nothing to conceal. Enlightenment was possible because of such a purified life and so much of determination and concentration. Buddhattva dawned. It may seem now that it dawned easily. It is not easy, it was not easy; it did not dawn easily, though now it seems to be easy. I now have eternal peace and internal tranquility, and everything lighted before me and was clearly visible, inside and outside.

That is the real reason that I expounded the Dhamma. I expounded it so well that none can reproach me. It is exquisite. It is a marvel. It is perfect. There is no flaw in it and hence none can say that because of this flaw or that weakness Dhamma is not well expounded. Dhamma is the best shelter. It leads one to Nibbāna. I have so well proclaimed Nibbāna that if it is practiced as it should be then any disciple can attain it in this very life and dwell in the taintless liberation of mind; liberation by wisdom. They will realize it for themselves by direct knowledge. Thus, Nibbāna is a marvel. It is bliss. There is no flaw in it. None can reproach it saying that it is not well proclaimed.

As there is no flaw in Dhamma or Nibbāna and as there is no such ground so I dwell secure, fearless and self-confident. When I depart – and I must depart someday – my departure will be secure, fearless and self-confident.

What is needed most is consciousness, alertness, meditation, meritorious deeds, concentration and self confidence. One must be alert all the time. Hence, one must get rid of drowsiness.

Alertness and Drowsiness

Drowsiness is sub-consciousness closer to unconsciousness. Alertness is consciousness; balanced consciousness that sees and feels the inner happenings and outer incidents simultaneously and with almost equal clarity.

Drowsiness is caused by non-acceptable and non-digestible ideas when the mind fails to understand something, and also when the mind is engrossed in altogether a different problem and the solution is not in sight.

The easiest way to get rid of drowsiness is to ignore the thought, not to give any attention to the idea that induces drowsiness. Drowsiness also vanishes when one starts thinking about Dhamma as one has learnt it and mastered it. Start examining it and investigating it closely. It also vanishes by loud recitation of Dhamma in detail. With some physical acts too drowsiness vanishes particularly when one starts rubbing the ear-lobes or the skin around the ears or temple or by pressing the big toes from both sides or by rubbing palms. The most popular way of getting rid of drowsiness is to get up, move a few steps, wash one's face and eyes and drink some water. Drowsiness vanishes easily. But the best way to get rid of drowsiness is to think of light and perceive light. When light comes to mind even when it is night and dark, the heart is filled with light and the mind is rejuvenated with the non-existent light which is contemplated upon and absorbed in a very subtle way. It is turning the senses inward. Then mind does not run wayward. Concentration increases and drowsiness vanishes. The last way is to lie down, lion-like, on right side, placing one foot on the other, keeping in mind the thought of rising. After awaking one should quickly get up and get fresh thinking that the pleasure of resting and reclining and sleep will take away precious time and ideas.

I have tried all these ways and a few more but have never allowed drowsiness to overpower me. These usually seem to be small things but it mars and disturbs the concentration and many precious ideas are lost through drowsiness. The loss of money and wealth is not big. The loss of ideas is indeed a great loss. Preserve, examine, store and follow ideas for betterment and refinement. I have often mentioned these things to my disciples. I have just shaken off drowsiness so it came to mind and reminded me of what I had thought and taught.

Drowsiness is just the opposite of excitement. If drowsiness is not good, excitement is also not good. By becoming excited, one loses self-control. If one lacks self-control then the mind will be very far from concentration. Success and failure are only gaining or losing concentration. Lose concentration at work and the work will not be finished; if finished it will not be good and useful. The completed work will lose its utility and attraction.

Contentious talks also produce excitement. One should train oneself not to listen to or indulge in contentious talk. It excites the mind and excitement dooms self-control. An uncontrolled mind is very far from concentration.

Companionship also gives rise to excitement. All companionships are not good but neither are all companionships bad. Hence, dwelling at a secluded place away from sound and noise, but full of cool breeze is far better for greater concentration and easy achievements; for higher thinking and refined ideas. Such places must be praised.

Free from Craving

One day, Mahāmoggallāna, my second chief disciple, asked me "O Blessed One! In what way can a monk be liberated through the elimination of craving? How can one reach the final stage, the final freedom from bondage and the final holy life; the final consummation? How one can be the foremost among devas and humans?"

I knew he was striving hard for Arahantship. A week after this teaching he achieved it by intense effort and sustained concentration. I said to him: '*sabbe dhammā nālam abhiniveshāya*; all things are not fit to be clung to. If a monk has learnt that nothing is fit to be clung to then he directly knows everything. By directly knowing everything, he fully understands everything. He knows and he feels the experiences. He is non-committed to everything whether pleasant or unpleasant, or neither pleasant nor unpleasant. Thinking so he concentrates, and thinks and contemplates on impermanence; dispassion; cessation and relinquishment. When he thinks of them and abides in them he does not cling to anything in the world. He is not agitated and personally attains nibbāna; and the feeling comes that birth is completed; that the holy life is lived; what has to be done has been done. There is nothing more in this world. He won't return to the world after nibbāna.'

Stress and Way out

I know stress. I have deliberately and painstakingly learnt stress. I know it and I have taught the monks and the laymen the noble truth of stress: Birth is stressful, ageing is stressful, death is stressful; sorrow, lamentation, pain, distress, and despair is stressful; association with unethical things and having none to care is stressful, separation from loved ones is stressful, not getting what is desired is stressful. Moreover, the five clinging-aggregates are stressful.

Once, I explained all these causes of stress and then addressed them:

"O Monks! This is the noble truth of the origination of stress. Craving makes for further becoming. Craving is always accompanied by passion and delight. One who has cravings, relishes now here this, and at another time there and that. One has craving for sensual pleasure, craving for accumulation, craving for becoming, and also craving for non-becoming.

The cessation of stress lies in renunciation and relinquishment, in releasing oneself from the shackles of craving by shaking off all the cravings. One can practice the Noble Eightfold Path for the cessation of craving. The Noble Eightfold Path of right view, right resolve, right speech, right action, right livelihood, right effort, right mindfulness and right concentration.

One must comprehend this noble truth of stress that vision arose, insight arose, discernment arose, knowledge arose and illuminated me with regard to things never heard of before. The origin of stress must be abandoned and the noble truth about the cessation of stress must be directly experienced to get rid of stress completely and forever.

I must make it clear that as long as my three-round, twelve-permutation knowledge and vision concerning these four noble truths as they have come to be were not pure, I did not claim to have directly awakened to the right self-awakening, unexcelled in the cosmos with its deities, Māra and Brahmas, with its contemplatives and priests, its royalty and common folks. But as soon as my three-round, twelve-permutation knowledge and vision concerning these four noble truths as they have come to be were truly pure, I did claim to have directly awakened to the right self-awakening, unexcelled in the cosmos with its deities, Māra and Brahmas, with its contemplatives and priests, its royalty and common folks. Knowledge and vision arose in me: Unprovoked is my release. This is my last birth. There is now no further becoming."

The Pursuit of Nirvāna

I have been teaching and showing the way, and making it clear how to move on that path: the Noble Eightfold Path. The aim is not the pursuit of perfection. The aim is the pursuit of Nirvāna, nibbāna, liberation, salvation, complete release from the cycle of birth-death and re-birth; no more birth. For all those that get nibbāna, that birth is the last birth and bliss.

In all these purifying and preserving the inner spirit is the crux, and a must for continuous and incessant ascent: higher and higher still.

But nibbāna is not so easy to achieve. I know, some monks who do not apply themselves to the meditative development of mind wish to get freed from the taints by non-clinging. Yet such minds won't be freed. Why can't such minds be freed? There is a definite reason for that. Such minds are not developed minds. They are not developed:

- In the four foundations of mindfulness;
- The four right kinds of striving; the four bases of success;
- The five spiritual faculties;
- The five spiritual powers;
- The seven factors of enlightenment and
- The Noble Eightfold Path.

I do remember and remember it well that I had given an apt and appropriate example of a hen which wishes that her chicks would break the cells of the eggs with their beaks and claws; and come out safe. But the hen has not sat on the eggs for an adequate period of incubation before hatching the eggs. As she has not sat over them sufficiently long enough hence, the eggs are not warmed enough; not developed enough. Despite the hen's wish, the chicks will not be able to come out. It is also true of monks who have not applied themselves to the meditative development of their mind; and thus they are not able to free themselves.

But if the hen sits long enough during incubation then the chicks will come out whether or not she wishes that her chicks should break the cells of the eggs with their beaks and claws and come out. It is true of such monks who have applied themselves to the meditative development of mind and whose minds are developed and mature. Their mind will be freed whether they wish so or not.

This inner development of the mind cannot be gauged every day, month or year, or even of a life-time. It is a subtle growth. Even the physical changes can't be gauged on a daily, monthly, or yearly basis.

While discussing it in another discourse I had given another very apt and appropriate example of a carpenter's axe or adze. The handle shows the mark of his fingers and thumb but the carpenter can't tell which mark came today and which one the previous or the previous month or last year. The marks that have appeared are the cumulative effect. Such is the case with meditative development. It cannot be marked or known on a daily, monthly or yearly basis but the mind develops and the cumulative effect of the development is easily experienced.

The totality of inner purification, meritorious deeds and inner developments results in nibbāna. Of course, it is difficult but since it is difficult, one must try to attain it. If one gets what is easily available, there is no credit to the mental agility and alertness and inner growth of the person. Credibility increases when one achieves something not easily achievable.

Short Life Span

There is another reason that one should try for it from the earliest possible time or when one becomes conscious of nibbāna or one comes to know about it. This reason is the shortness of our life. The usual span of human life is 64 years; the most cherished span is 100 years. One fourth of it is spent in childhood and learning. The 3nd quarter is most important as during this period we have utmost physical as well as mental strength. During the latter half, we are weak and keep on growing weaker.

That is the reason that a religious teacher Araka taught his disciples:

"O Brāhmins! Short is the life of human beings. It is limited and brief. It is full of suffering and tribulation. One must understand it wisely and do only good and live a pure life, for none who is born can escape death."

Let us assume that one lives for hundred years. Then, what are hundred years? They are equal to 300 seasons: 100 winters; 100 summers and 100 monsoons. In other terms, these are equal to 1,200 months: 400 winter months; 400 summer months and 400 months of rains. In yet other words, living that long a life is equal to 2,400 *pakshas*, fortnights; 800 fortnights of winter; 800 fortnights of summer and 800 fortnights of monsoons. If we reduce it to days; then living such a long life is equal to living for only 36,000 days: 12,000 days of winter; 12,000 days of summer and 12,000 days of rains. During that period one eats only 72,000 meals: 24,000 meals during winters; 24,000 meals during summers and 24,000 meals during the rains.

Half of that time is consumed by nights; a quarter of that time is spent in childhood and learning. Another quarter is spent in old age. What does one get? One gets only a few hundred days for working in physical health and mental agility and inner alertness. If that little time is spent in physical pleasure and luxury then one gets no time for inner and outer purification and to do wholesome and meritorious deeds.

This is what I calculated compassionately for the well-being and growth of my disciples. I have repeatedly advised them to meditate; not to be negligent to avoid more suffering and regret later on. If they follow my instructions they can be freed from clinging and attain nibbāna; total freedom.

Dhamma in Brief

The venerable Upāli wanted to know Dhamma in brief. Knowing Dhamma in brief is easy, but following those simple instructions is neither easy nor can be completed in a day, month or year. It is to be followed throughout a complete life.

One day, the venerable Upāli came to me and sat very close after paying respect and homage. I saw him and knew he had something in his mind. In order to give him an opening to express, what he wanted to say, I asked: "Venerable Upāli! You have come with a purpose. What is that purpose?"

Upāli said: "O Blessed One! If you teach me Dhamma in brief, it will give me very clear conception. Having heard Dhamma from the Blessed One, I might dwell alone, withdrawn, diligent, ardent and resolute. This may help me!"

Well, Venerable Upāli! It is not Dhamma in brief that is important; it is the right understanding of Dhamma that helps one in many ways. When you know certain things, they don't lead you to complete revulsion or to dispassion or cessation and peace or to direct knowledge, enlightenment and Nibbāna. Of such things you may think that this is not Dhamma; not the discipline or this is not the teaching of the Blessed One. But when you follow them meticulously for a long period, you know and feel that these things lead to complete revulsion to dispassion to cessation of suffering; to peace and tranquility, to direct knowledge, enlightenment and Nibbāna. Of such things, you feel and you are certain: this is Dhamma; this is discipline; this is the teaching of the Blessed One that leads to Nibbāna. Thoughts are important, meaningful and effective when they are converted into deeds."

Thoughts can be an Arhant to make it the last birth; a no returning state: *Sabbe prāptavantu nibbānah*!

HOMECOMING

A lot of commotion and an ever growing gathering has changed this lonely place into a fair. The colour, music and variety are being provided by the householders, particularly by the ladies and children. I'm still reclining and trying to take a nap. But there is a feeling that before that final great sleep there is no need of a nap. On the other hand, incessantly pouring in memories are not allowing drowsiness to come near me.

What I had to do before my final departure, I have already finished. The seed of Dhamma that I sowed one day is a fully grown tree now: large and wide; tall and deep; branched and leafy; and is yielding flowers and fruits, fragrance and delight and shade and energy.

I'm still waiting for water. I'm growing weaker and weaker. I know it is the time to depart. The final departure is essential. It changes an ever changing scenario. Whether felt of not, whether accepted or not, changes occur continuously without ceasing for a moment; without waiting for anyone or anything. Time waits for none. It is both a point and a period. Every moment we are at the intersection of different moments: both at the point of Time and in the period of Time. Time does not slip away from our hands. Time is abstract. It can't be touched, it can only be felt. I'm feeling the pulse of Time. I have felt the pulse of Time. I feel my own weakening pulse. It is time to depart.

My Nirvāna will be Mahā Nirvāna, Mahāparinirvāna. People are pouring in incessantly and the faces and scenario are changing every moment. Nature is changing. The sky is changing its colours; from one lovely colour to another lovely colour; with little clouds at some places and at the rest clean, cloudless sky: from deep red to yellow; from bronze to cream; from blue to pink. Oh! It looks lovely. Is Nature ready to take me back? Will the sky embrace me?

Yes, they are ready. I'm also ready after finishing all the work that I accepted on my own for me to complete before this awaited final departure, a journey of no return, a journey that goes on and on. I'm not trying to stop or evade the memorable moments that are pouring in my tranquil mind with similar speed. I'm looking at some for a few seconds, at others for a few minutes and then turning towards others. I cannot capture all those moments. They are living and lively moments. They cannot be ignored. One should not ignore such powerful moments full of vitality. I cannot and will not ignore them.

The Palace and the People

Oh Yes! Once, this was my palace. I'm again at the gates of that palace where I spent my very pleasant childhood and the first part of youth. How can a person forget his childhood and the attention and the people who loved him so deeply, from the very core of their heart? At least, a man like me, who remembers his previous births, cannot forget it. Why should I forget? There is nothing in my life that I would like to forget. There is nothing in my life that others would like to forget. People talk of my life and discuss my teachings. They have memorized those teachings. They will remember me. They must remember both my life and teachings. Both are important: important for cutting off the shackles and important for freedom from fear and suffering; and important also for making their current birth the last birth or a few births before the last birth. Then, there will be no arrival. It will be *parama ānand*, absolute bliss. It is for certain. It is true.

Many monks have come with me as they saw me turning towards the kingdom of my father. When I entered the capital city, people recognized me. They saluted me. Many men, women and children came out and stood in clusters. On the way ahead I found people standing on both sides of the road with flowers in hand. With folded hands they were all in *pranāma mudrā*. They showered flowers on me and on the monks who were accompanying me. I had not told them but they all knew where I was headed and experienced the importance of my homecoming. It is my first visit to my birthplace and the abode of my childhood and youth where I'm going again for the first time after I left that palace, and definitely it is the last time. Actually, I'm not returning but I am paying a visit. They deserve that visit. They have given me everything. I must share my enlightenment and wisdom with them. So, when I was close to Kapilvastu I turned towards the city. They deserve it and I must pay them that visit.

Once, I taught the big gathering one's debt towards one's parents. I remember that teaching. At that time I said:

"O Monks! Lay Disciples! Villagers! I declare that there are two persons whose debt can't be re-paid. They are the father and the mother. Even if one carries one's father on one's shoulder and one's mother on the other for a hundred years and attend to them by anointing them with salves, by massaging, bathing and rubbing their limbs, yet one would not repay them.

Even when one makes ones parents the supreme ruler of the earth; it would not be enough for the repayment of there debt that one owes to one's father and mother. The reason is very clear. Parents give life; bring up their children; foster them with tender care and guide them through this world.

But there is one who repays them adequately and even more than what one owes. He is the one who encourages his parents and establishes them in faith; encourages his immoral parents and settles and establishes them in virtue; establishes his miser parents in generosity and settles his ignorant parents in wisdom."

Showing the path to Nirvāna

I have come for that; for showing them the path. Though they are neither faithless nor immoral; yet I must show them the path of nirvāna.

The moment I reached the palace, I saw the king, queen, their family and the ministers coming out followed by others who were carrying baskets of flowers. They rushed to me and welcomed us by showering flowers. Rāhul was with his grandfather and Yashodharā with her mother-in-law. Ministers, officials and others were behind them.

Most of them prostrated before me; some of them touched my feet to pay their obeisance and homage to me very respectfully. There was no surprise in the homage paid by the younger generation; the surprise was in the homage paid by the elders. My parents were among them. Homage from elders was not new to me but these were the elders that had fostered me; carried me in their lap and on their shoulders. I thought over it for a moment. I realized that the homage is not for their child Gautam, it is for the Buddha, the Enlightened One; for one that has activated and set the wheel of Dhamma rolling; for one who has been teaching Dhamma, the way to nirvāna, the way to get rid of suffering and freedom from rebirth.

I said nothing but the thought of nirvāna kept my mind concentrated. I was not thinking what others were thinking. I was thinking about nirvāna.

Nirvāna is the ideal aim of human beings. They have born to strive for that. It requires constant spiritual exercise and contemplation. Before soaring higher into the subtle region of spiritual thought the aspirant cultivates the four noble thoughts: *Mettā* or universal love; *Karunā* or compassion; *muditā* or sympathetic inner joy or *uppekhā* or equanimity. These emotions and sentiments know no bounds of time, place, person or class. Universal love and equanimity are *pāramitās*, the perfections.

I am certain that I have come to show them the way to nirvāna. I will definitely do that. It has to be done here and now. It has been my intention in coming to this place, behind my homecoming. It would have been a mistake to think of all and disregard those who once looked after me with great care and affection. This is not the repayment of their affection. Affection cannot be returned. It is for my own satisfaction. As my wisdom is for all others, in the same way it is for them too.

My father, the king invited me to come inside and added that I must accept the throne. I smiled and politely refused: "I don't need it. I have other important matters to attend. I'm needed there. They need me. I will obey the call of conscience."

They were so emotional that they wanted to weep but did not weep. They were apprehensive that if they wept, they would not be able to hear me clearly.

A high seat was given to me outside the palace. I sat on it and looked around. Oh! Every inch of the large and wide space was filled up. There were only people everywhere. Still, many persons kept coming. Yet another wonder was that despite such huge crowd there was virtually no sound. No one spoke. All of them were looking at me: intently, eagerly and with expectation.

When I had taken the seat, the royal family members led by the king came very close to me and expressed their wish to enter Dhamma. I was about to announce my acceptance but there was a great roar from the crowd from every side. All of them were speaking simultaneously and in a similar, very loud tone. It was not musical. It was cacophonous, very harsh to listen. It took me a while to understand that all of them, men, women, young, old; were expressing their wish to enter Dhamma.

Yet I asked the king, my father: "What is all these noise and commotion about?

"O my dear son! O Blessed One! Oh Enlightened One! The people of the whole kingdom want to enter Dhamma. They have been repeatedly demanding this. But I had ample faith in my son that you would come to me at least once before I die. So, I waited for you; the whole family and also the whole kingdom waited for you. They have got what they cherished and wished to get for many years.

O Enlightened One! O my dear son! Accept me as a disciple of Dhamma."

"O Yes! Wisdom has dawned on me! I became the Buddha and expounded the Dhamma! I accept thee unto Dhamma," I said in my normal voice.

Mother came forward. She was Mahāpajāpati Goutami. She has given me the name 'Gautam'. She seemed to be the happiest one. She was weeping and smiling. She was not able to speak clearly yet I heard her very clearly. She said with folded hands, "I was very worried son! They said you had become weak, lean and thin! No, no! You are very strong; far stronger! Take me to your fold! Accept me unto Dhamma!"

"With the blessings that I received I became the Blessed One! I accept thee to Dhamma." My mother became the first women to be ordained into Dhamma.

Rāhul had caught Yashodharā's right hand. She freed herself and with folded hands touched my feet. Rāhul too followed her steps. Then, both of them stood there with folded hands. After a long interval Yashodharā was able to say: "Accept me unto Dhamma!"

"Me too!" said Rāhul, almost simultaneously. Yashodharā pulled him close and pushed him towards me saying: "Your son unto your Dhamma. He should be on your path. It has been my wish."

There was no attachment, no weakness and no emotion. I was normal. I said in the same normal voice: "Yashodharā! I accept thee unto Dhamma!

Rāhul! I accept thee unto Dhamma!"

First I signalled to the crowd to be silent, though it was now only a low sound that was coming. When complete silence was restored again, I decided to teach them many different things.

Then, the time-consuming work of ordination began. It was both personal and community initiation. When that function of initiation was over, from inside the palace, some people came out with big baskets on their heads. They went in different direction and with the help of others, began distributing food in bowls made up of leaves. I stopped speaking and waited for them to finish their work. When the basket was empty they went inside and brought more food. All were served food.

Insight into Dhamma

The work of distributing food was over. During that period there was a bit of disturbance. Then, they gathered again around me and sat silently and expectedly. I knew they wanted to hear something. Then it came to my mind and I almost repeated what I had expressed in a discourse at Sumsumāra Giri in the Deer Park of Bhesakalā Grove. I said:

"O Lay Disciples! And Monks! At this time of the initiation of the King, Queen, the royal family, the ministers and personnel in royal service, and that of the people of Kapilvastu, I will tell you, for whom is the Dhamma and for whom it is not. It is for eight types of good men and it is not for that many types of men of opposite qualities. Which eight? For whom is the Dhamma and for whom it is not?

- The Dhamma is for one who has few wishes. It is not for one who has many wishes.
- The Dhamma is for the contented. It is not for the discontented.
- The Dhamma is for the secluded. It is not for one who loves company.
- The Dhamma is for the energetic. It is not for the indolent.

- The Dhamma is for one who has a concentrated mind. It is not for one who lacks concentration.
- The Dhamma is for one who possesses vigilant mindfulness. It is not for one of lax mindfulness.
- The Dhamma is for the wise. It is not for one who lacks wisdom.
- The Dhamma is for for him who seeks delight in the unworldly. It is not for one who obtains delight in the worldly affairs.

The crowd silently and patiently heard me. Though, I could not see all their faces, yet whomsoever I was able to see, I saw a lot of satisfaction on the faces of the people present there. I explained what is meant by all these types. I said:

"Why has it been said that Dhamma is for one who has few wishes and not for one who has many wishes? A person can have certain qualities but he may not wish to make those qualities known to others. In this sense, a person is a man of few wishes.

Why has it been said that Dhamma is for the contented and not for the discontented? There can be a man who is contented with whatever food or shelter or clothes he gets or in whatever circumstance he lives. It is in this sense that a person is contented.

Why is it said that Dhamma is for the secluded and not for one who loves company? A man that has work to do cannot waste time in idle talk with different persons. He is a man of action and deeds which are more important than mere words. So, a man meets others and talks only a little to dismiss them and proceeds towards his work and workplace. It is in this sense that a person is secluded.

Why is it said that Dhamma is for the energetic and not for the indolent? It takes a lot of physical and mental energy to resist temptations and lead a balanced life. That person has great energy who abandons everything unwholesome and performs only meritorious deeds. It is in this sense that a person is energetic.

Why is it said that Dhamma is for one who has a concentrated mind and not one who lacks concentration? A person acquires *gyān* in stages, which comes only when he has concentration and can meditate over a single point for a long time. It is in this sense a person has concentration.

Why is it said that Dhamma is for one who possesses vigilant mindfulness and not for one of lax mindfulness? A person is mindful, possesses the keenest mindfulness and circumspection, so he remembers what he has said and done earlier. It is in this sense that a person is mindful.

Why is it said that Dhamma is for the wise and not for one who lacks wisdom? A person is wise when he is able to see the rise and fall of phenomena; is noble and penetrative and succeeds in complete cessation of suffering. It is in this sense that a man is wise.

Why is it said that Dhamma is for him who seeks delight in the unworldly affairs and not for one who obtains delight in the worldly affairs? A person's mind encourages him to proceed towards the complete cessation of suffering, which is *papanchā nirodha*. This is nibbāna. It is in this sense that a person takes delight in the unworldly."

Lay Disciples

Then, after a long pause, I explained what was meant by a lay disciple. I said:

"How is one a lay follower? When one takes refuge in the Buddha, the Dhamma and the Sangha, he is a lay follower. How is a lay follower virtuous? When a lay follower abstains from the basis for negligence, the destruction of life, from taking what is not given, from sensual misconduct, from false speech and from consuming intoxicants, wines and liquor, the lay follower is virtuous.

And how does a lay follower live for his own welfare but not for the welfare of others? If a lay follower has immense or even simple faith, virtue, good conduct and generosity in himself but he does not encourage others to have faith, immense or even simple, virtue, good conduct and generosity, he lives for his own welfare and not for the welfare of others. If a person himself likes to visit monks, listen to Dhamma, learn the teachings, retains them in mind, examines them carefully, understands deeply and follows confidently, and if he himself lives in conformity with the Dhamma but does not encourage others for such living; does not encourage others to do so, then that lay follower lives for his own welfare and not for others.

And how does a lay follower live for his own welfare and also for the welfare of others? If a lay follower has immense or even simple faith, virtue, good conduct and generosity in himself and encourages others to have faith, immense or even simple, virtue, good conduct and generosity, he lives for his own welfare and for the welfare of others. If a person himself likes to visit monks, listen to Dhamma, learn the teachings, retains in mind, examines it carefully, understands deeply and follows confidently, and if he himself lives in conformity with Dhamma and also encourages others for such living; and also encourages others to do so, then that lay follower lives both for his own welfare and for the welfare of others."

The discourse was over but I had to say a lot of things: everything that had happened after my departure from the palace and my homecoming this day. I kept on speaking but I did not say all that I wanted to say. Different thoughts were coming and vanishing. One of them was a question: would the story and details of my struggle, meditation and penance be helpful to these people? The answer was very clear: my teachings would, but the struggle wouldn't help them get rid of pain and suffering.

The king once again asked me to step inside the palace to stay there but again I refused politely. Then he requested me to stay very close to the palace in the Banyan Tree Monastery. I agreed and we came to that place. Many people followed us. It was a big and open place. We stayed there.

Self-examination

Quite often I begin self-examination; introspection of the self. It starts in a natural way, I think neither about introspection, nor do I make an effort. It starts effortlessly. The mind gets a link and with that link it sees the complete scenario that had appeared before the eyes in days past. I re-live the moments that come alive. The conversation is heard clearly and a different meaning is drawn without the search.

It gives a lot of inner satisfaction to know the mind of others but it gives far more pleasure and satisfaction to know one's own mind. It is just like looking into a clear mirror. Men, women, youth and those fond of ornaments and makeup prefer to look into the mirror and if they find even smallest alien particle, they will pick it up and throw it out to keep their face and body clean. It is like that, if one looks at one's own mind and finds even a bit of dirt, he or she cleans it up. It is cleansing mind. When the mind is clean, it is satisfaction, pleasure and bliss.

Self-examination is very essential as it is helpful in the growth of wholesome qualities. One must ask certain questions for self-examination:

- Do I have ill-will often in my heart or am I often free of it?
- Am I often covetous or often free from covetousness?
- Am I often immersed in torpor and sloth or am I free from them?
- Am I often excited or tranquil?
- Do I use insight in knowing my feelings or not?
- Am I often in doubt or free from doubts?
- Do I often suspect others or look at others with a clean mind?
- Am I often angry or free from anger?
- Is my mind defiled by unwholesome thoughts or is it free from defilements?
- Is my mind often restless or free from restlessness?
- Am I energetic and active or lazy and inactive?
- Do I often examine thoughts or never examine at all?

- ❖ Do I listen to my conscience or ignore it completely?
- ❖ Do I follow moral bindings or ignore ethics?
- ❖ Am I full of desires or have I got rid of them?

If one asks such questions and examines the self one can be clean and pure and perform only meritorious and wholesome deeds. *Nissaraniyo dhātuyo*; they offer an escape from the adverse or obstructive state of mind. This way, one can grow faster and better. I addressed the people and monks sitting there and made them understand with clarity by saying:

"Four kinds of persons are found in the world:

Persons going with the stream;

Persons going against the stream;

Persons standing firm; and

Persons, who have crossed over and gone to the far shore, are brāhmins who stand on dry land.

Of what nature is the person going with the stream? He is one who indulges in sensual desires and commits wrong deeds.

Of what nature is one who goes against the stream? He is one who does not indulge in sensual pleasure and commits no wrong deeds. He lives a holy life but in struggle, with difficulty, aggrieved, sighing and in agony.

Of what nature is one who stands firm? He is one who has destroyed the five lower fetters. He is due to be reborn in a celestial realm; remains there and gets final nibbāna from there.

Of what nature is one who has crossed over and gone to the far shore, a Brāhmin who stands on dry land? He is one who has destroyed the taints. In this very life he enters and dwells in the taintless liberation of mind, and the liberation of wisdom. He has realized it for himself through direct knowledge.

You may be in the first stage of being or in the second but you must meditate, examine and grow to the fourth state. That is the aim. Everyone must try to attain that fourth state."

Before leaving the life of palace, I had examined my mind deeply and in detail. I made my decision and went out to accomplish my aim. I know I don't need to examine my inner self because my whole life has been clean and pure, and I have done only meritorious and wholesome deeds. Yet I examine it. It helps in reading the minds of others. I am tranquil, balanced and at ease because I know that all things are rooted in desire; having risen from *gyāna* produced by contemplating on *ashubha*, foulness, one directs one's mind towards a sensual object in order to examine it; just as one who has taken an antidote examines poison. Things rooted in desire come to actual axistence through attention. They originate from contact and converge on feelings. The foremost of all things is concentration. All things are mastered by mindfulness. Wisdom is their peak and liberation is their essence. All these are co-related with *bhāvanā cha vibhāvanā cha*; with *buddhi-vināsha*, growth and decline and *sampatti-vipatti*, success and failure. All things merge in the deathless, and Nibbāna is their culmination.

Chanda-mulukā sabbe Dhammā; the five aggregates come to be through the cravings of the previous life, which is brought about in the present existence. *Manasikāra-sambhavā sabbe Dhammā*; The world of objects becomes present to consciousness only through *manasikāra*, attention. *No cha assa, no cha mey siyā; na bhavissāmi, na me bhavissati*: It might not be, it might not be mine; it will not be me and it will not be mine; if there were no defilements and *kamma* in the past, there would not be for me at present the five aggregates; so there will be no defilement and in future there will be no renewal of the aggregates. This mantra could lead to no returning, the deathless state, Arahantship and Nibbāna. Apparently, deathless state and Nibbāna seem to be synonymous but there is a fine distinction: in the deathless state, the Nibbāna element remains and is left as a residue, but in Nibbāna no residue is left. If there is some residue of clinging one will attain the stage of no returning, but if there is no residue left then one will acquire the final knowledge in the present life.

Therefore, I said to them that the way to nirvāna is very straight and easy to move on provided that one has purified oneself; has no desire, lust, anger or jealousy; is pure of thought, mind and deeds; examines and meditates with deep concentration for attaining different stages of *gyāna* in order to attain Arhantship and nirvāna.

For the liberation of mind I also explained them *Mettā-chittovimutti*. Mettā the loving kindness that I had got from them and the wish for the welfare and happiness of all living beings.

When I was staying there, Mahāpajāpati Gautami, with her entire large family and attendants again approached me. She paid the homage and said:

"O Buddha! The Blessed One! Please teach me the Dhamma in brief, so that having heard the Dhamma from the Enlightened One, I might dwell alone, withdrawn, diligent, ardent and resolute."

When they had settled down very close to me I said: "O Gautami! You know of certain things. These things lead to passion, to bondage but not to detachment; to accumulation of material wealth and things for luxurious living but not to diminution; to greater desires, not fewer wishes; to discontent and gregariousness but not to contentment, satisfaction and seclusion; to indolence and extravagance but not to frugality and greater flow of energy. This is not Dhamma. That which leads to dispassion but not to passion; to detachment but not to bondage; to diminution but not to accumulation; to withdrawal but not to indulgence; it leads to fewer wishes but not to a discontented state and to greater energy but not to indolence and frugality, is the Dhamma. Of such things one can be certain. This is the discipline. This is my teaching."

At the end, after a week-long stay and daily discourse, when I was leaving the place, the garden and palace with the monks, I wished them all happiness and wisdom; welfare and peace and health and nibbāna.

HIGHER VIRTUE; HIGHER MIND AND HIGHER WISDOM

Once I compared the training for higher virtue; higher mind and higher wisdom with the refinement of gold. A monk, who is virtuous and is restraint by the *Pātimokkha,* finds danger in the slightest faults. He is perfect in conduct and resort. He knows the training rules and follows them. He then acquires training in higher virtue.

Four States of Gyāna

In the same way a secluded mind, secluded from sensual pleasure; unwholesome states and deeds, one that has completed training in seclusion acquires training of the sphere of higher mind. A Monk so trained in seclusion enters and dwells in the first *gyāna.* This state is accompanied by thought and examination; with rapture and happiness, which is born from seclusion. After thought and examination have subsided, he enters and dwells in the second state of *gyāna,* which gives internal confidence and unification of mind. This state is without thought and examination and is accompanied by rapture and happiness born out of deep concentration. When the rapture fades away, he gets equanimity and becomes mindful. His comprehension is clear. He experiences happiness with his body. Then, he enters and dwells in the third state of *gyāna.* When he succeeds in abandoning pleasure and pain, he enters and dwells in the fourth state of *gyāna.* This fourth state is neither pleasant nor painful. It shows the purification of mindfulness by equanimity. It is the training in the higher mind.

A monk or lay person then understands the truth as the reality really is: that this is suffering; this is the cause of suffering; this is the way to cessation of suffering and this is the cessation of suffering. This is the training in the higher wisdom. The higher wisdom includes the wisdom of insight, which leads to the super-mundane path.

Such training frees one from lust, hatred and delusion. One then abandons everything unwholesome and never resorts to any evil.

Refinement of Gold

This training in higher virtue, higher mind and higher wisdom is akin to the refinement of gold. It is not confined to only refinement of mind but adds to the virtue and wisdom too. It brightens the existing state.

When gold is mined out of the earth and sand or river, it contains soil, gravel and grit and has gross impurities, like our general life. The goldsmith or his apprentice pours the impure gold into a trough and washes, rinses and cleans it thoroughly. Even after that cleaning and rinsing, the gold contains moderate impurities. The same process is repeated again and again. Only after repeated washing does pure gold remain and impurities are washed away. Yet, the gold is not entirely pure.

Seekers try again and again to be pure and every time they feel that some impurities are left in them, they try again. And yet, all the impurities are not removed. There should be no *Pamāda* or *pramāda* or moral laxity, which is lack of mindfulness and persistence in the pursuit of self-purification.

For making the gold totally free from impurities, the goldsmith or his apprentice pours the gold into a melting pot, smelts it and melts it together. But it is not immediately taken out of the pot as the dross has not been entirely removed. So, the process is repeated again and again and a time comes when all impurities are removed entirely and the gold is quite pliant, workable and brighter. Then the goldsmith makes whatever ornament he wishes to make.

It is also true of monks and other seekers. They are devoted to the training in higher virtue, higher mind and higher wisdom. They repeat the process and every time they come out brighter. It is done again and again. All the bad conducts of body, mind, thought, speech and deeds are rinsed out and cleaned. There are no sensual thoughts; thoughts of ill-will and violent thoughts are completely erased. Every such thing is abandoned, eliminated and abolished: *kām-vitaka; byāpāda-vitaka* and *vihinsā-vitaka*, the three wrong thoughts are thoroughly shaken off.

Yet some taints are left there, at least regarding thoughts about higher mental states experienced during meditation. The attention is not yet peaceful, tranquil and sublime. But with constant and sincere practice a time comes when the mind is inwardly steadied, concentrated, composed and unified. Calmness and refinement mark this state. It is the final state of abandoning evil and cultivating good. There is no evil left. There is then only goodness. Then, *Dhamma-vitaka*, agitation about the higher state is also abolished. The seeker has achieved *sati sati āyatana*, which is the preliminary condition for the attainments of *abhinnā*, six-super-knowledge. Five of these are mundane and the sixth is supra-mundane for the attainment of Arhantship. It is *āsava-khaya*, the destruction of the taints and not their suppression. It comes after the mastery over the fourth state of *gyāna*. Like the pure and bright gold, our life is also brightened when the impurities are dusted away with meditation and wholesome deeds.

If such things are attained then immense energy, *dhātu*, virya; rises in three stages: *ārambha-dhātu*, the element of arousal is the first arousing of energy; *nikkama-dhātu*; the element of persistence is the second stage when energy overcomes indolence; and *parakkama-dhātu*; the third element of energy as exertion. It is the most advanced stage when energy becomes indomitable and invincible.

Tathāgata

All these combined together endows one with enlightenment and makes one a Tathāgata like me. Why am I a Tathāgata? Who is a Tathāgata? It is *tatha āgata*, one who has come thus, through the same path of practice, attainment and enlightenment that the Buddhas of the past came. If the syllable is broken in another way then it is *tathā gata*, one who has gone thus; one that has gone through the same path as other Enlightened Ones have gone. The very word Tathāgata makes it clear that the person is fully released from the world. It is known to a majority of people.

The Tathāgata understands the world, and the origin of the world is abandoned by the Tathāgata. It has been fully realized by the Tathāgata. The cessation of the world and the path of cessation of the world are fully realized by the Tathāgata. He has developed the path of cessation.

The Tathāgata fully understands whatever is there in the world Devas; Māras; Brahmā; ascetics; Brāhmins; humans and others that are seen in the world, heard, sensed, attained, searched into, and pondered over by the mind. He is conqueror and unconquered. That is why he is called the Tathāgata.

There is one person whose arising in the world is for the welfare of the multitude; for the happiness of the multitude. He comes into the world out of compassion for it, for the good of the world and for purification of the immoral and faithless. He is the Tathāgata.

The Tathāgata is unique, without peer, without counterpart, incomparable, unequalled, unrivalled and definitely the best among the humans.

The manifestation of the Tathāgata is the manifestation of great vision; of great light; of great radiance. Tathāgata is the Arhant; the fully Enlightened One.

The Tathāgata speaks, utters and proclaims from the day of his perfect enlightenment up to the day when he completely passes away into the nibbāna element without any residue left. Therefore, he is called the Tathāgata.

The Tathāgata speaks, so he acts, as he acts so he speaks. Therefore, he is called the Tathāgata. That is why I am the Tathāgata.

It is very clear that such a state is attained through struggle, unremitting struggle with resolve. The seeker gets the power and ability and capacity of getting, realizing and attaining everything through direct knowledge and gets nirvāna.

Pukkusati

Among many faces and many places one tender face in a shed comes to me again and again. The innocent, childish, pure and determined face of Pukkusati appears repeatedly for a few seconds, goes out in robes and alms-bowl and then vanishes. The same appears again in the small shed where I saw him for the first and last time. He was a disciple for a few hours. I gave him the needed and essential teaching. He absorbed it and became an Arhant and departed into Parinirvāna. From there, no one takes birth again. More than my teaching his own purity of thought, words and deeds metamorphosed him into an Arhant.

It was destined. Before meeting him I had no idea. He was waiting but he did not know. We did not know each other. Yet I went there, received his introduction, gave him the teaching and he went out for his robes and alms-bowl. He had no need of them, so he changed into a deathless state; a no returning state and departed. But I see him in the shed of a potter.

I entered the shed of the potter to stay there. A Bhikhu was staying there. He was a young and bright Bhikkhu of tender age; full of the glow of purity. I did not know him. I had not seen him. I liked him. He too looked closely and intently towards me because of my appearance. He had so much of inner purity and power that I was instantly attracted towards him. I thought, and was sure that the young recluse possessed higher virtues and higher mind. He only lacked higher wisdom, which is essential for nirvāna. I decided to give him higher wisdom. I asked the young recluse:

"O Bhikkhu! In whose name have you left home? Who is your master? Whose doctrine do you follow?"

The young recluse kept on looking at my face then answered politely: "O Friend! There is a recluse Gautam, a Shākyan scion, who has renounced all and left the Shākyan royal family to become a recluse. It is all known around that he is an Arhant, the fully Enlightened One. He is my master. I follow his doctrines."

It was a delightful experience. I was sure he did not know me. He had not heard my sermons. Yet he was following my doctrines. I asked: "Where does the Enlightened One live at the present moment?"

"He is at present in a city called Shrāvasthi in the north," the young recluse replied.

I placed a straight question: "Have you ever seen this Blessed One? Would you recognize him if and when you see him?"

The young Bhikkhu replied: "No! I have never seen the Blessed One. I may not recognize him even if I meet him."

His truthfulness and purity appealed me. An element of wonder was there because here was a young man who had left home to become a recluse in my name and is quite unknown to me. He does not know me. He accepts me as his master without even having met me. I was overwhelmed by different feelings. I announced:

"O Young Bhikkhu! I will teach you the doctrine. Listen and pay attention. Here it is:

Then I taught him elements; detachment; *Uppekhā*, equanimity, the way towards the attainment of higher spiritual state; to become Arhant in order to attain nibbāna. I focused on purification and showed him the sphere of infinite consciousness, which is the sphere of nothingness. From there on, one can develop the power of mental creation through annihilating *vibhāva* and becoming *bhāva*. This comes from perception. Perception comes from sensation. Sensations can be pleasant, unpleasant or neutral. All sensations are impermanent. These experiences do not bind us.

I explained him absolute wisdom, the knowledge about the extinction of all desires. I said:

"O Bhikkhu! *Mosadhamma*, unreality is false; *Amosadhamma* is Nirvāna, the Absolute Truth, *sachcha*. Therefore, a person so endowed is endowed with Absolute Truth. This *param ārsha satyam*, the Absolute Truth, is reality and Nirvāna.

Then Pukkusati realized that the person sitting before him and teaching the doctrine is none other than the Blessed One. He had seen, realized and understood the Absolute Truth. He was beaming both with knowledge and with reverence for me. He rose up, came to me and prostrated: "O Blessed One! Please forgive my ignorance. I did not recognize you and like a fool, addressed you as 'Friend'. Please ordain me and admit me into the order of the Sangha."

I knew he was in the state of an Arhant and had a very short stay here on the earth, in that form. He was to depart to deathless state for not coming again. I asked:

"Are you prepared for it? Where are your robes and alms-bowl?"

"Yes, I am ready to enter the order of the Sangha. The alms-bowl and robes are not ready. If you allow me then I will go out and make arrangements for robes and alms-bowl."

I gave him permission and he departed. I remained there, sitting still, waiting for the news. Some people came to me. The potter was also among them. He said, "O Bhikkhu! An angry animal attacked the recluse Pukkusati, who was staying here and mortally, injured him. He has succumbed to the severe and serious injury."

I stood up. The innocent and pure face came before me. I looked at the small gathering and declared: "Pukkusati was pure. He had learnt the Absolute Truth. He had become an Arhant. He has departed never to return to this world."

Decades have passed. Off and on, his face has been coming to my mind. Today, when I am myself ready to depart and enter nirvāna the face is appearing before me again and again. I liked that face, its purity and fuller inner growth. I liked his concentration and truthfulness. It changed him into an Arhant. He has returned home, the infinite home, never to return to the earth again.

MAHĀPARINIRVĀN

I'm still lying in the Kushinagar forest recalling past events and explaining them to myself. Numerous living and lovely moments are pouring in incessantly. I look at some, remember a part of some but I have no time and hence, I'm not ready for all of them because it is the day of my Mahāparinirvāna.

When I reached 80, I decided to leave the earth and this earthly body, after 45 years of intermittent journey and regular teaching and after imparting wisdom and knowledge of the path of nirvāna to numerous individuals.

Some two months back I decided and declared to enter Mahāparinirvāna within a short time. That time has come. I must be ready for my final departure and move towards infinity, eternity, timelessness and deathlessness from where I will not have to return to earth and life again. I am ready.

It is the day of Mahāparinirvāna. Parinirvāna implies a release from the Bhāvachakra; Samsāra; Karma and Punarjanma or rebirth. It also implies the dissolution of the Skandhas. Mahāparinirvāna implies the same thing, but that of the Enlightened One. It is a voyage of no return; a one-way journey.

Activities Around

From a distant place the high pitched sound of *Nagārā* has just started booming. It is the biggest drum and its sound covers a vast area. The villagers are announcing my departure. It means, people from other villages will also hurry to this part of the forest. Oh! They show respect but actually they love me a lot.

The sound of the *Mridanga* too has begun its beat. It is coming closer, accompanied by the flute. I know the villagers are coming in groups to welcome me and to celebrate my departure. Yes, this departure must be celebrated.

In close vicinity swans have started their cry-song and a peacock has begun its dance on the lowest thick branch of a nearby tree directly before my eyes. I can't miss it. Even the peacock is not willing to miss the last sight. Birds have always been very close to me.

Hundreds of parrots have come simultaneously and have covered one tree completely. They are jumping and flying from branch to branch in ecstasy, but are making no sound. A few starlings also came into view occasionally and then went out of sight. They were playing some game. After a long interval the coos of cuckoos were heard. A very large curve like a bow of herons was visible once in the sky. It passed over my head and towards the river. They have made their presence felt. I noticed them when they were directly before my eyes. They were flying very high. They may have seen the big congregation and continued their flight. They knew the importance of the occasion.

The trumpet of an elephant is matching the sound of the *Mridanga* and S*inghā*. I think many *Mridangas* are being played simultaneously on *Kaharawā tāla*. Someone has started playing the *Veenā* and it is the *rāga Mālkauns*. From behind, the drumbeat in *teena tāla* was coming without break. Some women were singing some folk song in chorus and the sound was coming closer and closer. One thing was very uncommon that the men gathered there were not talking. At least, the sound of any conversation was not reaching me. The music was both engrossing and illuminating. The drum players were experts. They were not missing any beat. The occasional trumpet of an elephant was getting mixed with the similar sound of the *Singhā*. The players must be large in number. Perhaps a whole *tolā* of *Singhā* players is coming with their curved musical instrument.

For a moment, two pairs of deer were seen but I did not see them again. They must be resting at a distance in some bush. They know all the places where they can take rest or hide from the hunters. Deer has always been very dear to me.

Nature was fully absorbed in whatever was happening there; and so many things were happening there.

It is a pleasure, boon and bliss to enter Parinirvāna amidst classical music by human beings and natural music by trees and birds.

The Last Meal

The villagers have started pouring in. One of them is Chanda. He is a blacksmith by profession. He had brought some mushroom delicacies for me. He offered it to me. I accepted it. I liked its smell and ate half of it. My need for water was communicated to the villagers, who had come with fresh water. But I had drunk some dirty water too. I was not at ease. Within an hour my condition began deteriorating. I heard one villager accusing Chanda, "What did you give? The Muni has not digested it." I did not hear Chanda but I felt that he must be worried. I thought over it.

I fell terribly ill. The illness was for all to watch and learn. Food sustains both body and mind. I instructed the monks near me:

"Go and assure Chanda that the food offered by him has no connection with my departure. It was announced two months back. I am ready to enter nibbāna of my own volition. Tell him and announce to all that the meal offered by Chanda should be considered of the greatest merit, as it is my last meal. I will eat no more and depart finally within a short time."

I had fallen ill with a definite plan. The illness is only in appearance. Through it I must teach the world that life is not permanent and death is obvious, so one must strive for nirvāna. Nirvāna must be the highest goal of every human being. If all human beings make even a minimum effort to get it, then humanity will become a sublime entity: wise, meritorious and a saviour.

I don't know whether others marked it or not but like the gathering of human beings, the animals that had gathered in the vicinity were also not making any sound. Even if they were, making some sound it was inaudible. The occasional sound of the trumpet of an elephant or the cooing of some cuckoo made their presence felt. Otherwise I'm sure other people were not thinking of them. On the contrary I am thinking about everything, every bit of movement, even from my back or beyond my sight is coming to my mind. It is in the most active state. My mind is conscious of everything and everyone.

I could smell a very enchanting smell; the mixed smell of flowers, fruits, humans and animals. A light wind was spraying the fragrance and spreading it all around. At times, I could feel different fragrances.

The monks and the villagers wanted to construct a shed over me but I asked them not to do so as the trees were doing that work and the whole of the sky and the complete space was visible. A shed would have taken away that broad view.

I remembered the sheer vastness of Nature and my long and close contact with her. I have spent more time with Nature than anywhere else. I know Nature and she knows me. She fascinates, infatuates, purifies and enriches. Her lap is soothing and warm, cozy and comfortable. Her incessant music flowing everywhere has pleased and pacified me. Glowing dawns and alluring evenings have enchanted and enthralled me. The ponds, lakes and rivers have quelled my fatigue; the humming bees and chirping birds have drawn my attention. I won't stir when the birds and butterflies are playing around me. I never did disturb them.

Nature's fascination is always pure and sublime. The vast and open fields and surroundings have bewitching and magnetic, magical and enchanting beauty. Human, plants, animals, even insects and the Devas are captivated and enticed by the provocative and innovative glamour of long stretched farms, green plants of equal size and similar make and wild flowers. I feel infinity with and am delighted by Nature and natural appearances. I have been filled with mixed and varied smell of flowers, fruits, soil and plants. They have enticed and invited me and I have preferred to be with them. They have nothing to hide. They offer everything. Whatever one gives to Nature, one gets back manifold.

Completion of Works

But even the memories of those sights have not been able to keep my condition stable. Nothing can! It is deteriorating and the condition will keep on deteriorating for a few more hours and then it will attain total and complete stability in *nirvāna*. Then there will be no body and no deterioration. Then the journey will stop; stop for ever. It will acquire no re-start. It has been a definite and destined journey, not a casual one.

There has been an axis and axle of *Karma* that has determined the pace and direction of the journey. On that axis and with that axle it was free to move slow or faster but till today, the separation was not possible. The freedom was entangled with the wheel. But the time has come to be free as I have done everything that I had to do in my last life here on earth. There is no work left. Hence, there is no need of any more birth. The requirement is over. The teaching has already been given and repeatedly repeated at different places. The monks have memorized them and repeat them exactly in my words, but with a different tone and tempo. They teach and the lay disciples are also themselves learning them. These teachings will keep on giving light, building character and showing the path to nirvāna for many millennia after my final departure. It is Mahāparinirvāna today, No *kamma* is left, no residue is left. It is complete. The fulfillment is perfect. The wisdom attained through enlightenment has been spread like light; fragrance and delight.

It will last forever and everywhere. It will not remain limited to the places that I visited or to the regions where I delivered the sermons and definitely not limited to the present disciples. It will be there at distant places in yet to be born disciples and in the very distant future too.

The cosmos and Nature have their own say, fixed course and flexible ideas. Mahāparinirvāna will stop one way of living, thinking and doing and start another way of living, thinking and of virtually no doing. At another point of time I will enter another period of time, but this time I will enter into timelessness. Nature creates and saves. It retains and reproduces at the right time at the right place and during the right season. This righteousness is immortal.

Either the villagers have brought flowers or there is a garden nearby, as the fragrance of flowers has filled the nostrils and the milieu. The light wind is bringing it; different and from different sides. The wind is not coming from one particular direction. Yet it is not a whirlwind. It is soothing, fragrant and rejuvenating. The soothing, refreshing fragrance of *champā, chameli* and *kanaka* occasionally fills the nostrils, goes deep down up to the navel, and levels stability to my condition, impetus to my thinking and sharpness to memory, and adds value to the incidents.

There is movement all around me. I felt a lot of activities were going on, yet there was no noise. Everything was very smooth and natural. People were moving but there was no sound of movement. The movement of light indicated the movement of the people. They were very busy. If they had to talk something they were going far away from me to keep me at ease and free from any sort of disturbance. I was not disturbed. I was not feeling any disturbance. It must be the idea in the minds of the busy-looking monks and sad villagers. They should not be sad, they should be happy. It is the happiest moment.

Stability: Durability: Immortality

Ānand came late. He must have had some intuitions and then decided to follow my path. He must have started the next morning and is therefore many hours behind. Immediately after his arrival he protested against the Mahāparinirvāna on the pretext that the place is a forest and inconvenient. He requested me to postpone it and announce another day and place for my Mahāparinirvāna. The remote jungle of Kushinagar was not fit for it. I reminded him of the glorious past of the place which was ruled by the Mallas.

I know this *Shāl-van* is the best place for my Mahāparinirvāna. I was born under a tree, I played and grew in a palatial garden, I roamed in natural surroundings, I attained enlightenment under a *peepal* tree; I delivered my first sermon in the *Mriga Vātikā* in the open under a different tree; I have delivered most of my sermons sitting under different trees; and hence, this is the best place for Mahāparinirvāna.

After that, Ānand said nothing about it but was worried. He tried to give me as much comfort as was possible.

The message through the *nāgārās* was being continually sent. The people were coming. The gathering became massive. I asked the monks and the lay disciples and the villagers to clarify their doubts if they had any; to ask question as it is the last chance that they would get for it. They looked at each other but no one said anything. No one came forward with any question.

Ānand was sitting silently, very close to me. I gave my last sermon to him:

"Be an island unto yourself, Ānand! Be a refuge to yourself; do not take to yourself any other refuge. See truth as an island, see truth as the refuge. Do not seek refuge in anyone but yourselves. Have heart, Ānand! Do not weep, do not distress yourself! Have I not often told you that it is in the very nature of things that we must eventually be parted from all that is near and dear to us?

For how, Ānanda, can it be otherwise? Since everything born and organized contains within itself the germs of disintegration, how can it be otherwise then, that a being should pass away? No other condition is possible!"

For long you, Ānanda, have been very near to me by acts of devotion, faithfulness and affection, ever loyal beyond all reckoning. You have been teaching others and looking after me and my needs. You will ably teach the Dhamma. You will surely teach and show that there is no stability, no durability, and no immortality, as I have taught and shown.

The Devas, gods and demigods have approached me again as they had approached me after the Enlightenment and had gathered to listen to the first sermon, Dhamma Chakka Pavattana. They have witnessed the rare moments and listened to rare teachings and are present at the moment of a rare event. It has been destined, so they knew it. They want to speak, to say something; maybe to ask something but like others, they also are not speaking. They must be feeling that their words and sound may disturb me. No! Nothing can disturb me. I am firm. I am stable. I have endured and shown durability and in my death I will establish immortality. Living before death is not, but living after death is immortality. It must be accepted and made known.

Eternal Words Covering Eternity

At the last moment when I thought of departing, I remembered what I had often repeated, *jātasya hi dhruvo mrityuh*, he who has taken birth must die. As my last words, while ready to depart I said: "All composite things pass away. Strive for your own liberation with diligence."

The light increased. The gathering vanished. The *shāl-van* vanished. The trees, birds, animals, flowers, trees and human beings vanished. The light kept on increasing. Then it was only light. Then I saw the wheel. It was the wheel of light. Light was not coming from it, it was made up of light. There appeared a lotus with ten thousand petals; a lighted lotus. Each petal was lighted. Light was not coming from the lotus, the lotus itself was light. It was only light. And there was light: in me, outside me and around me. It was all light. I became light. Life is light. Life is the petals of divine lotuses. Life is fragrance. Life is a cycle, a wheel. Life is everywhere. Each life has different and many cycles: cycles of this moment; current year; this life and other lives.

It is the wheel

It was the same light that I had seen at the time of enlightenment; the same glow; the same brightness, an infinite light spreading towards everywhere up to infinity. I was illuminated so much that I was light. Light was not coming from me or from anywhere else. It was I who had changed into light.

The wheel had started moving. It had a rhythmical pace. The lotus started moving, matching its pace with that of the wheel. The light moved. It also moved in a similar rhythmical way. I started moving like the lotus, the wheel, the light. I am moving with the same rhythmical pace. I am one among them. I am with them. I am all of them.

The wheel is moving. I am moving. The wheel is eternity. I am the wheel, I am eternity. I am on the lotus. The lotus is moving. It has covered me, usurped me. I have become the lotus. I am the lotus. The lotus is eternity. I am eternity. The light is moving. It is me. I am moving as light. The light is eternal. I am eternal.

I am eternity. I am eternal. Eternity and Eternal! Eternity and Eternal! Eternity and Eternal!